ON THE TRAIL OF BADEN-POWELL

H ALLEN ROSE

On the Trail of Baden-Powell
Copyright © 2020 by H Allen Rose

All rights reserved. No part of this publication may be reproduced, distributed, or transmitted in any form or by any means, including photocopying, recording, or other electronic or mechanical methods, without the prior written permission of the author, except in the case of brief quotations embodied in critical reviews and certain other non-commercial uses permitted by copyright law.

Tellwell Talent
www.tellwell.ca

ISBN
978-0-2288-2262-2 (Hardcover)
978-0-2288-2260-8 (Paperback)
978-0-2288-2261-5 (eBook)

Table of Contents

Acknowledgments v
Prologue vii

Tales From The Twelfth Troop
    Winter Camp - Sutherland Beach 3
    Winter Camp - West Bank North of CP Train Bridge 8
    Beaver Creek 12
    Drinkle's Bridge 14
    The Spitted Chicken Caper 17
    The Sand Dunes 19
    Coyotes 21
    24th of May Swim 23
    First Aid - Don't Leave Home Without It 25
    The District Commissioner and the Legion Dinner 27
    The Cigarette Caper 29
    Happy Hollow Sex Education 31
    The Bottle Drive 34
    The Hoop Dance 37
    Archery in the Church Hall 42
    Gilwell Training and the Wood Badge Beads 45
    Christopher Lake 49

Aborted Moves
    The Log Cabin at Spy Hill 55
    The Feeder Operation 58
    The Red Tailed Hawk 61
    Toby 65

Vienna
    The Parents Day Hike 71

Ottawa Adventures
    Charge Certificate 79
    The Tay River Run 82
    The Big Log Campfire 87
    The Beaver Pond 92
    The Lost Cub In The Cedar Swamp 95
    The Bobcat 98

Mississippi Bloopers
    Canoe Tripping 103
    The Mis-read Rapids 104
    The Low Level Campsite 106
    Raccoons 108

Acknowledgments

I first have to acknowledge the help of my son Peter Rose, retired operator of Canada's NRU nuclear research reactor in Chalk River ON, for his patience and hours of computer time converting my writing into something my publisher could work with.

The photographs were copied from a pamphlet called Soaring High, put together from the log book of The Senior Scouts of the 12th Saskatoon Troop by Sam Horton in 2003, one of those seniors and a retired Vice President of Ontario Hydro. I was the Scouter in the last days of those Seniors before adulthood took over our lives.

Then of course my publisher Tellwell Talent Ltd of Victoria BC for taking on the task of producing this book and convincing a very old, retired and computer illiterate engineer that it could be done. Their patience must have been stretched at times, but they never let that show. Unfortunate that they were not available thirty years ago when I wrote this as a retirement project. Publishers at that time were not interested in new amateur writers.

Without the Boy Scout movement that Robert Baden-Powell created back in 1931 much of this story would not have happened so I sincerely wish the movement a long continued worldwide future.

Prologue

Who was Baden-Powell? Lord Baden-Powell started the world wide youth movement known as Boy Scouts. His wife soon followed with the creation of the Girl Guides. All the thousands of leaders since, men and women, and all the boys and girls who have grown up in the movement have, in one way or another spent their lives on the trail of Baden-Powell. The basic message was simple. Do what's right. Give it your best shot. Learn to stand on your own feet and have fun while you are at it.

I have spent most of my life associated with the Boy Scout movement and my memories are ones of high adventure. Of course every troop is different and every meeting does not produce memorable events, but such events come to any troop that rises to the challenge of scouting. Most of them happen on camps and this book is largely a collection of camp anecdotes from thirty years of active camping. This is not a "how to" manual, but rather a collection of incidents which make up some of my best memories; memories which everyone who has gone through the scouting experience is bound to share in one form or another.

The Movement started with Lord Baden-Powell, the famous defender of Mafeking, who, on his return to England wrote a manual which he called Scouting For Boys. His motivation was to bring some training and adventure to city boys who he saw as having little objective or excitement in life. He based his book on the skills exhibited by native boys in Africa who helped the military defence forces at Mafeking as couriers and spies, often risking and sometimes losing their lives.

Scouting started then with distinct military overtones. These were retained in the United States and dispensed with in Canada and most other countries over time, but the basic experience for boys was similar regardless of the philosophies behind their supporting institutions. Namely to learn how to take care of yourself in the outdoors and to stand on your own feet and be a responsible citizen in whatever circumstances arose. And above all, to have fun doing it.

Because of the time in the century, the female equivalent, Lady Baden-Powell's Girl Guides was a very different activity, aimed at producing good future wives for the men that the scouts would become. This is not to criticize the Girl Guides, but it would have been nice if the original movement could have been "Scouting for Kids", male and female, an absolute impossibility in the England of 1908.

My experience with combined girl\boy activity, including camps, was always a good experience. These are kids ranging in age from twelve to sixteen and the presence of both sexes always resulted in improved performance from everyone. And more fun. Most boys of that age are too self conscious for good campfires, while girls seem to revel in the singing and the creation of skits and games. They were always able to drag the boys into the spirit of the thing, which rarely happened without them.

However, most of Scouting has been a segregated business, so these anecdotes perforce relate only to boys. I would hope that there are similar stories in the annals of the Girl Guides and if someone writes them down I'd be only too happy to read them.

I started in Cubs in the Saskatoon 12th Pack at Grace United Church in 1939. I remember very little of that experience because the Pack folded after my first year. It started up again in 1941 but by that time I was scout age and joined the 12th Troop. It was a rough troop. The boys all came from the Eastern outskirts of Saskatoon and were only barely civilized. I'm not sure why that was because Grace Church was in one of the better districts and quite far from Albert school where most of us came from. In any case, we were there first and the more domesticated boys avoided us.

The Scouter was a dedicated man with a good heart. He wanted to uplift us all, to take this scruffy pack of jackals and make good citizens of us. He succeeded to some degree but wasn't willing to give up on anyone and some of those guys were lost causes. That wasn't his downfall though. We spent a lot of time camping and he was always cold. The cure for that was to share a sleeping bag with one of the boys every night. Now I shared his bag on occasion and I know there was nothing homosexual about the arrangement. But someone mentioned it to their parents and that was the end of that Scouter. Incidentally, he married a couple of years later and had children, so what can you say. Group committees don't take chances.

We had another Scouter for a year who also tried to deal with our gang with mixed success. I'm sure we were just the type of kids Baden-Powell had in mind originally but turning into good citizens just isn't for some people. After another year he was transferred to Prince Albert and then we got the Scouter that I remained in touch with till his death in 1993

Skipper, James Albert (Bert) Bowron 1900 to 1993

Skipper was the title he adopted and that's what everyone called him. He was a retired physical training instructor from the armed forces and a war was on. Tough! We started out each meeting with grass drill. He could do 46 one armed push ups with either arm and he was sixty five years old.

Skipper had no illusions about saving any bad eggs. His objective was to have the best troop in the province. Shape up or ship out. Well, some of our guys were just rugged individualists and were not going to conform to anyone's system. I was the oldest scout at the time and sort of the leader of the rat pack. We spent a year with Skipper throwing people out and me arguing them back in. I lost, and the worst of the delinquents disappeared, but Skipper was impressed by my obstinacy and made me the Troop Leader. I didn't have the qualifications but he soon took care of that.

We never quite agreed on the philosophy of the thing. Skipper's theory was that you had two choices. You could have a good troop by selecting the good boys and weeding out the losers, or you could try to save the bad ones and have a poor troop. I always tried to save the bad ones but not to the extent of jeopardizing the troop. I nearly always lost.

I finally faced the truth that all you can do as a leader is offer a program that you are good at. Keep the boys that like what you have to offer and let the rest go. Scouting is not the only option in life and a lot of boys do just great at other things. Of course some never find a path to follow. Que sera, sera.

Under Skipper's leadership the troop blossomed. We had the first Senior Scout patrol in Canada. This was an idea imported from England to make room for promotion of younger boys to patrol leaders if the older ones decided not to leave the troop when they reached the age of sixteen. Two of that senior patrol became senior vice-presidents of Ontario Hydro and I finished my career as Director of International Relations for Atomic Energy of Canada. Skipper and his approach to life played a considerable part in those successes.

After three years Skipper was transferred to Regina in February. The Group Committee asked me if I would take over temporarily until they could find a new Scouter. I was eighteen. Eight years later I was still running the troop and doing my best to follow in those large footsteps. I never got past five one armed push ups.

Skipper had two principle activities that he based his programs on. Camp craft and Indian lore. Canadian Indian culture was his hobby and that and camping fit exactly with the basic Scouting objectives.

Skipper and the Teepee

The visit of Vilhjalmur Stefansson to Saskatoon in 1945 inspired the idea of camping in the winter in Skipper's head. He obtained an army manual on winter survival and when I had all that learned he started us on winter camping. He never went. He said I needed to develop self reliance and sleeping out at minus thirty without his help was just the ticket.

So that is the background for all the stories that follow. I haven't included names because I never retained records of all the troops and my memory for names isn't up to that. The stories aren't chronological either, and maybe the facts get twisted a bit here and there. This isn't a history book. What bothers me is that I am sure there are many other stories that have slipped my mind and that I would enjoy remembering and sharing with whoever would listen.

A word about winter camping. It is not for amateurs. If you don't know what you are doing you can die out there. Surviving outside at minus 30 isn't especially complicated but you won't survive mistakes. No margin for error is the rule. If you are tempted to try it, the November and December 1986 issues of "the leader", the magazine published for Canadian Boy Scout leaders, has an excellent feature on winter camping. I wrote it. The specific reference is volume 17, numbers 3 and 4 and copies can be obtained from Canyouth Publications Ltd., PO Box 5112, Stn. F, Ottawa, Ontario, Canada, K2C 3H4.

Surviving Canadian cold requires avoiding five basic threats. Cold, wind, wet, hunger and exhaustion. It is nothing more than common sense, the one sense that twelve year olds lack.

Cold is handled with insulation. The trick is to know what kind and how much. Artificial heat is out. If you need a fire to keep warm you won't survive more than one night, especially on the prairies where finding enough fuel to cook with can be a problem.

Wind is obvious to anyone who listens to wind chill readings on the weather forecasts. While travelling, wind proof clothes are the only solution. In camp you must find a spot protected from even light breezes or manufacture a wind break however you can. Don't count on snow unless you are sure there is enough hard packed depth to make walls out of. Cedar swamps make great wind shelters in winter but deciduous trees and other evergreens are useless, except as supports for fabric windbreaks.

Hunger and exhaustion are pretty obvious.

The big one is the wet. It is incredibly difficult to keep dry outdoors in winter. Try leaving your clothes on when you get home from a vigorous cross country ski some day. You will find a chill creeping up on you very soon and that is inside the house. It comes from evaporating sweat that you didn't even notice you had. Outside, that evaporation can sap your body heat faster than you could believe once you stop moving. If you are damp when you make camp you have to strip down to the skin and put on dry clothes. When you go to bed you have to strip down to the skin and crawl into your minus thirty sleeping bag dry. It only hurts for a minute if you do it fast.

Where boys get into trouble is snow in the clothes and sweat. They like to wrestle in the snow, throw it at each other, stuff it down each others neck. Allow them to do this and you have real trouble coming up.

Enough for the warnings. Do your homework before trying sleeping out in the winter. One other absolute rule. Make the first sleep out in someone's back yard. If you get into trouble the house is right there. If that goes alright then you can try the bush, but stay within reach of help until you are sure the boys know what they are doing.

Tales From The Twelfth Troop

Winter Camp - Sutherland Beach

The twelfth Saskatoon Troop was a camping and outdoors troop. In the war years, summer vacation seldom meant more than a cessation of school for most boys and probably an extra load of chores around home, like weeding the potato patch. Summer camp was the only real break a lot of kids got and it was usually at a lake or out at the Beaver Creek scout camp fifteen miles south of the city.

Winters in Saskatoon are long and the idea that one should know how to survive one outside started, I believe, with the exploits of the North Pole explorers. At one point, Vilhjalmur Stefansson visited Saskatoon on a speaking tour and all of the troops in the city went to hear him. Our Scouter, who went by the title of Skipper, was a retired army physical training officer and followed up with a booklet he obtained from the army that described the essentials of winter camping. It wasn't long before we decided to try it.

Skipper had no experience in this sort of thing and no one had any equipment. In fact the equipment one thinks of now had not even been imagined. Wool was the only insulating material available and sleeping bags were made by folding and pinning an 8 point Hudson Bay blanket in such a way that it kept in sufficient heat to survive a night in the open. If you did it wrong there was a good chance you wouldn't see morning.

Why did parents allow us to do this? That's something I never understood. I guess it demonstrates the remarkable reputation the Scout movement has enjoyed, and deserved, over the years. I suppose there was also a feeling born out of the agonies suffered by the troops in two world wars that your son's chance of surviving might be enhanced if a third one ever came along.

Skipper obtained some surplus army frame packs. These were the latest in high tech equipment at a time when sporting backpacks were non existent, and they allowed a 40 kg boy to carry enough insulation and food on his back to survive a one night outing. Our first trek using these packs was out to Sutherland Beach, a bend in the Saskatchewan River about 5 k north of the city and about the same distance West of the small town of Sutherland. We always stuck to the river or the Beaver creek valley because they were the only source of firewood and the only hope of finding shelter from the prairie wind.

No one went to Sutherland Beach in winter so there was no road. We also had no skis or snowshoes, which made a 5 k hike through drifted prairie snow a considerable ordeal, particularly with packs weighing nearly as much as we did.

Author with Two Senior Scouts

Weather forecasting at the time was still the preserve of the indians, and we didn't know any indians, so we never had a very good idea of what lay in store. Cold for sure and maybe wind and snow. Not to worry. We knew what we were doing.

I was the troop leader at this time and at the age of sixteen or so was entrusted with the lives of boys who had passed all the requirements our Scouter laid down. He was 65 and was past sleeping out in the winter with only a Hudson's Bay blanket. No tents. We couldn't carry them even if we had them and they don't help much at minus 20 anyway. It doesn't rain in Saskatchewan in the winter. Sometimes not in the summer either.

On this particular trek their were six of us, the senior patrol of the troop and all capable campers. No sloppy bedrolls in this group. The day was clear and cold but calm and we left Grace church in high spirits. We were taken to the ski jump beside the dam on the north side of the university and took off across the snow drifted fields, across the Canadian Pacific tracks and along the river bank towards our destination some 5 k away. Five k doesn't sound far but prairie drifted snow is not easy terrain and you have to avoid working up a sweat if you don't want to freeze later. The snow packs in waves across the prevailing wind, hard pan to the windward and soft in the lee. You walk two or three steps on top and then whump! Up to your knees in soft snow. Struggle to the next wave, climb three steps on top and whump! It took all day to make that 5 k.

The snow in Saskatchewan is not usually deep and when we got to the beach we were able to clear a fire spot fairly easily and prepare supper. The beach is not exactly sheltered. There were no buildings of any kind. Willows without leaves don't provide much of a wind break but they make great cooking fires and with full stomachs we were looking forward to the night with only slight misgivings.

The sky was a funny milky colour to the north but there was no wind, and stars started to show when the sun went down along with the temperature. Well, we expected to suffer so when nine o'clock came we burrowed our blanket rolls down into soft snow and crawled in, wriggling and bouncing to make a hip hole before the snow beneath us turned to ice. Why nine o'clock? Because the sun doesn't get up till about eight in the morning and eleven hours on an ice mattress is quite enough to suffer through.

Sleep comes quickly after a day like that and you want all you can get before the cold starts to seep through and the ordeal of waiting for first light begins.

With that expectation in mind, it was with a vague feeling of apprehension that I awoke. Eyes suddenly wide open, listening. Nothing but the ringing in my ears. Pitch black. Then something else came through. I had to relieve myself badly, but I was unexpectedly warm. The two things don't go together on a winter camp.

The thought of climbing out to pee at probably minus thirty kept me in place for a few minutes and the unearthly silence became more unsettling. I had never heard silence like that and the feeling of apprehension grew.

Well, nature always wins and I finally poked my head out from under the blanket only to be met with a shower of snow in my face. The second try was worse and then I came to the realization that it was hard to move at all. Finally, in a sort of panic I threw the top of the bag back and scrabbled out into a small avalanche of snow wearing nothing but long johns and a pair of socks. It was full daylight.

Of the five others there was no trace. A dazzling expanse of white was all that was to be seen. It had snowed 30 cm overnight in a dead calm and the blanket of white lay unbroken by so much as a rabbit track in all directions.

Now snow is a great insulator of heat and sound and my companions were not likely to wake until the call of nature drove them out, as it had me. I burrowed back into my bedroll to retrieve my clothes and dressed, trying desperately to keep as much snow as possible outside. Not easy when loose snow kept rolling in as fast as I could scoop it out. I thanked God there was no wind. I then dug out the fire pit, found the wood we had stacked the night before and got a fire going and a pot of sweet tea brewing.

Now to get the rest of the crew up. But where were they?

I tried to remember where everyone had bedded down and cautiously ploughed my way towards where I thought Fred lay. I didn't want to step on him. God knows what he'd do, waking up buried with something standing on his chest, or somewhere worse. I didn't want to start with a wet bed to contend with.

Then I noticed something in the unbroken surface. A small hole about big enough for a mouse. As I watched a little wisp of steam rose from it. It was an air hole just like a hibernating bear would make. We had seen these before on top of beaver lodges and there was no mistaking what it was.

I carefully scooped snow away until the top of Fred's bag came into sight and then carefully lifted the blanket to let in the light. Fred's head slowly emerged, eyes blinking in the sudden light exactly like a hibernating bear emerging in the spring. Then the snow collapsed and Fred came scrambling out with a string of words not found in the army manual on winter camping.

Once Fred was dressed more or less dry we repeated the process with the other four. The tough decision was who to wake last, because that one wouldn't get to see the little air holes and would feel hard done by. We finally decided on one of the Frost twins, thinking somehow that the other would somehow pass on the experience in some magical fashion. After all they were identical. Unfortunately the second twin didn't see it that way, but what can you do?

Breakfast was a bit of an ordeal, wallowing in snow up to our waists, trying to keep the fire from drowning in meltwater so we could cook what was left of our rations. Our problems were not over. We still had to cover five k through that waist deep stuff with the same prairie drift waves underneath that had been so tough on the way out.

We didn't want to leave anything but we also didn't want to carry more than necessary. There were two Oxo cubes and a can of condensed milk left. Rather than pack them, Fred ate the two cubes like candy and then drank the condensed milk straight while the rest of us gagged.

By noon we got to the CP tracks pretty well done in and could see the ski cabin another half k away. Then the rest of the horrible truth hit. No vehicle could get through to the cabin and we would have to plough our way on foot another three k to the university before any hope of rescue materialized.

Skipper was there at the end of the ploughed road by the Chemistry building. He claimed he had just arrived, having estimated exactly how long it would take us to get out. To our cries that we might have died out there, he just laughed, pointing out that the physical, mental, psychological and spiritual training he had given us was more than sufficient to deal with any crisis whatsoever. The funny thing is we believed him.

Winter Camp - West Bank North of CP Train Bridge

I only had one small disaster winter camping, and I didn't really understand why until I got old myself, and lost my resistance to cold. People are not born equal. Some have much more resistance to cold than others. Until I passed fifty I was almost insensitive to cold and I never understood the complaints of others about being chilled to the bone. Insulation that keeps one person comfortable can lead to hypothermia in another. Each person has to find out for himself how much protection he needs.

This camp was our most ambitious yet. Fourteen boys, some not quite fourteen yet but all second class scouts who had passed their first aid and winter camping tests. One of the younger boys had been in a house fire and had scarring over half his body. Scar tissue is not as good as skin and we were a bit nervous about him, but he had slept out in his back yard unscathed so we decided to let him come along.

This camp was to be across the river from Sutherland Beach, about where the present sewage treatment plant is now. We had picked that spot because it had fairly dense willow growth and afforded some shelter from the wind. The trail started at the ski jump and went from there over the CP train bridge. The bridge had a side walk so it was not dangerous except for the wind, which could really get to you on a cold day. Mind you a train going by was only two feet away and it was not a pleasant experience to share the bridge with one.

I had a key to the ski club cabin so we grouped there to start the trek. The sky was clear with a brisk north west breeze which was standard fare in Saskatoon in those days. No sign of snow but obviously a cold night coming up.

Everyone was equipped with either snow shoes or skis and an assortment of foot wear that included moccasins, ski boots and unfortunately rubber boots. Rubber boots have to be propped open at night or they freeze so solid it is not possible to put them on in the morning. I had moccasins with me to wear in camp, but in the morning I had to give them to the rubber boot boy who couldn't get into his boots. I therefor started the morning in ski boots which offer very little in the way of insulation and are an invitation to frostbite unless you are skiing. They are not camp wear.

The trek was not exactly pleasant, the wind having got to everyone by the time we got off the bridge. There was nothing but bald prairie there at that time so we had no protection on top of the river bank either. We opted to go down to river level to get out of the wind but of course the snow drifts down the bank on the west side and the going was pretty heavy. It warmed us up but also played us out.

The advantage was that by the time we reached camp there was no time for anything but supper and digging in for the night. After the bedrolls were laid out we tried a hike out on to the river to study star constellations. The wind had quit but the temperature was dropping at a rather frightening rate and was already minus twenty fahrenheit. That's about minus thirty centigrade. It wasn't long before we decided to retreat to the relative warmth of the sleeping bags.

The boys had wisely agreed to bunch together this time, rather than each making his own solitary nest. It also gave more space to stand and undress without getting snow into everything. It took a bit of persuasion this time to get them to strip down and put on dry clothes before crawling into the bags but they all finally did it.

Once the boys were safely tucked in I and my assistant and the troop leader made our own way to bed some twenty metres to one side. It's always best to give the boys some space so they can talk among themselves without worrying about some adult criticizing their topics of conversation.

The night passed without much sound coming from anybody, but I was uncomfortably cold and my assistant was obviously not getting much sleep as he rolled and tossed, trying to find a position that kept in the most heat. It was just getting light when one of the patrol leaders grabbed my shoulders and started shaking me.

"Scouter! scouter! Billy's frozen solid." I scrambled my head out into the weak morning light and picked my small thermometer out of my ski boot. The instrument read down to minus thirty Fahrenheit. The liquid was all in the bulb at the bottom.

I didn't wet my bag but it was a close thing. I dressed in record time, partly from fear but mostly from the air which froze anything exposed almost instantly. By the time I got to the boys sleeping bags I could hear Billy crying. Thank God. Not frozen solid. I put a hand on the bulge int the middle of the blankets.

"Billy. Scouter here. Can you feel your feet?"

"Yeeessss! (wail) They huuurrrt!"

Thank God again. Not frozen if he can feel them.

"All right guys. Up and at 'em. I need your blankets to get Billy warmed up. And dress fast. It's forty below out here. Dress and pack up. We'll go back to the ski cabin and light the heater and have breakfast inside."

The promise of heat got them moving and in half an hour we were on our way back to the cabin. There is rarely any wind at that temperature so once on the move everyone warmed up. A watch for frozen noses was all that seemed necessary. Learning-the- hard-way experience coming right up.

We got back to the ski cabin about eight o'clock and Doug Worcester, the club president was already there with the place heated up. He was already preparing to come rescue us when he saw us on the bridge. I guess he had looked at the temperature at bedtime and hadn't slept very well after that. Doug owned an old Model T Ford and mixed kerosene with the oil so it would start even at forty below. At that temperature it doesn't make any difference whether it's centigrade or Fahrenheit.

I had started the bacon and eggs for the whole troop when my assistant called me over.

"Listen to this Al." He stamped his feet on the cement floor. Clack, clack, clack.

"Your moccasins are frozen Fred. Take them off and hang them above the heater."

"I can't feel anything when they hit the floor and clack like that."

I stared at him and he wasn't joking. I sat him down and unlaced one of the moccasins. It was frozen to his sock. I started to roll the sock down and about the instep I found the skin black. I rolled the sock back on and told Doug. We agreed that it would be a mistake to do anything except get him to the hospital. Thank God again for the Model T.

We then checked everyone's feet, but Fred was the only casualty. I asked him why he hadn't said anything out on the trail. Standard procedure is to take the boots off when frostbite threatens and warm the persons feet by putting them on someone's bare stomach. He claimed he had no idea that they were freezing until he heard them clacking on the cement floor.

I know now that you can freeze feet without knowing it's happening, particularly in ill fitting snow shoes that may cut off the circulation to the toes. But that was too late for Fred. He spent two weeks in hospital and lost all the skin from both feet, but happily not the toes themselves. They never fully recover though and he is stuck with cold-sensitive feet for the rest of his days. And I am stuck with a guilt complex for the rest of mine.

Beaver Creek

The Saskatoon regional scout camp was twenty five kilometres south of the city on Beaver Creek. Beaver Creek flowed from the Blackstrap over by Dundurn, through the military base and on into the South Saskatchewan River. It was the most ideal campground you could imagine in a region of otherwise unbroken prairie, sand dunes and flat marginal farmland. It was also the only one within easy reach of the city. The creek had cut down through the prairie sod and maybe 20 or 30 meters into the sand long enough ago that the slopes had settled into gentle rolling hills covered with a forest of silver willow at the brink, merging to poplar farther down and finally to diamond willow lining the meandering creek.

The creek attracted all the wildlife indigenous to the area, beaver of course but mule deer and jumpers as well; bush rabbits and jack rabbits and gophers and the predators that lived on them, the coyotes and badgers and weasels. South of the creek the land was desert for several miles. Real Sahara type desert with nothing but sand and prickly pear cactus. Once over the first dune you could imagine yourself in the middle of the Kalahari. People got lost and occasionally died out there. The stuff that boys imaginations turn into major adventure.

After a big wind the bottom of the dunes would scour down to hard pan which would be littered with the bleached bones of small animals that had died there, unable to climb the steep banks of sliding sand. Sometimes there were arrowheads among the bones, beautifully crafted points for arrows and spears, and sometimes white men's artifacts, lead slugs from the old forty fives and the even bigger slugs of the buffalo guns. It wasn't hard to imagine the wars between indians and cowboys that had taken place there, even if it had never actually happened.

The creek meandered as prairie streams do. I suppose the scout property was no more than three miles long, if that much, but the length of creek in that space was at least three times that distance. It was really a string of small swimming holes separated by narrow channels overgrown with diamond willow. Most of the scouts in Saskatoon had a staff made of diamond willow. For the boy with the patience to carve and polish the diamond shaped blemishes that covered the two inch thick trunks, the result was a natural work of art unequalled by any human hand.

There were enough of these meanders to give one to every troop in the city for their own territory. It makes a tremendous difference to a boy if he is looking after his own ground rather than space he thinks is someone else's responsibility. Kids have an instinct to defend their own and attack their enemies, usually anything that appears to be officially adult.

The adult world seldom appreciates the value of things like Beaver Creek. Back around 1950 the military decided they needed more room and annexed the whole of Beaver Creek. End of an era for Saskatoon Boy Scouts. Scout officialdom in Saskatoon never uttered so much as a whimper and neither did city council. Most of them were ex-military. We had just finished world war II and nobody questioned military decisions.

Drinkle's Bridge

I knew Beaver Creek from the time I was a little kid. My parents summer holidays were spent on a farm that the creek ran through, living in a tent and cooking on a camp fire; fresh eggs and cream and chickens roasted over the coals; a creek to explore that was full of frogs and small fish and garter snakes and mosquitoes. We ran nearly naked all summer and our feet got so tough we could walk on cinders and never feel it. No one worried about ozone or skin cancer in those days. In today's terms we were poor but I didn't know that. Life was good. So when I was old enough to be a Boy Scout, Beaver Creek was already a second home to me and to most of the kids on our side of town.

So what about Drinkle's bridge? Dr. Drinkle was an engineering professor at the University of Saskatchewan and wanted to do something for the Boy Scouts. Now one of the great things about Beaver Creek was that it was narrow in between the pools. After the spring flood there was no current in it and you could safely build boy scout bridges like they showed in the scout manual. Of course our constructions left a lot to be desired and few of the bridges ever survived the next spring flood. We had to rebuild them every year, which was just great. Every year a new set of scouts got to build bridges under the supervision of last years bridge builders. The technique never improved because scouts grow up and leave before they can become really good at anything.

Typical Scout Bridge

Dr. Drinkle and the official scout bureaucracy went out to the creek one day to see what could be done to improve the place. Perhaps a headquarters building (one was eventually built). The thing that struck Dr. Drinkle, the civil engineer, was that our bridges were a disaster. More often than not, crossing one of them resulted in a dunking in the creek when it collapsed, particularly when a whole troop decided to test the resonant frequency by bouncing up and down in unison.

The decision was made on the spot that a proper bridge would be a great improvement to the site. There was some excitement among the troops at the prospect of learning how to build a real bridge. Its location was a point of discussion too because the area was divided up among the cities troops and each one had its own bridge.

Nothing happened for some time though and scouts, whose attention span is short at the best of times, forgot about the bridge. Until one day we went out to camp. There were tread marks of heavy machinery across the prairie going towards the creek. Curious, we followed the tracks down the hill and through the trees and there it was. A brand new bridge. Concrete footings, steel cable trusses and massive beam deck that could carry a truck.

No scout had even seen the construction let alone participated in it or in the design or in the decision about placement. Of course it was in the headquarters area. The one thing that puzzled headquarters was that scouts were seldom seen on the bridge. Until the army booted us out we just kept building our old rickety bridges on our own campsites and took the dunking when they collapsed as one of the great pleasures of camping at the creek.

The Spitted Chicken Caper

Our Scouter in the days when I was troop leader specialized in dreaming up fun things for the troop to do. He was a typical Brit and an ex-army physical training instructor, so his ideas were somewhat extreme. Not surprisingly, many of his boys became athletes. He was also a nut on native indian lore, but that's another story.

This particular idea was for each boy to get a chicken (already dead, thank God), pack up his gear for an overnight, cycle out to the creek, (which was our only means of transportation at that time), construct a spit over a fire pit, build a fire, spit the chicken, roast it and have supper. Just the chicken. No potatoes and gravy.

I was working so I and my younger brother were going to bike out after work. No problem. Skipper said there would be lots of chicken left over and we wouldn't have to cook our own.

Now cycling with a full pack for twenty five kilometres over roads that are only gravel or sand filled ruts is not that easy a go. Kids are pretty tired and hungry by the time they get there. Then nobody knew exactly how to build a spit that would last long enough to roast a chicken.

It took a couple of hours of experimentation before the chickens were finally a-roasting. Of course you can't leave a spitted chicken to roast while you go and play. You have to squat there for two hours slowly turning the spit and keeping the fire just right so the thing cooks without becoming a burnt offering, and with no refrigeration they have to be well cooked. No eating it half raw!

By the time I got off work and we cycled out to the creek it was already dark. The camp wasn't hard to find. We saw the glow of fires and heard a sort of rumble of voices long before we got there. It was a scene from an African safari movie. There was Skipper cornered in his tent with the troop gathered in a threatening crowd around him brandishing sticks. He had two drumsticks clutched behind his back which he was trying to save for us. There wasn't another scrap of chicken in the place. Even the smaller bones were gone and he had confiscated breakfast, knowing they would need that for the ride back to the city the next morning.

We took our drumsticks and ran off into the night to eat them in the safety of darkness, listening to the ravening crowd searching for us in the night.

The Sand Dunes

The sand dunes south of Beaver Creek have to be seen to be believed. I don't know how far they extend, but certainly far enough that you could die if you became lost. Like any true desert, the temperature gets hot during the day and cold at night. In Saskatchewan getting lost is a remote possibility if you know anything at all. The sky is seldom overcast, the sun is always south at noon, southeast in the morning and southwest in the afternoon. At night the big dipper and the pole star can't be missed and the creek runs east and west. Just go north and you can't miss it. If you don't hit the scout camp, at least you have water to drink.

One of the favourite adventures at the creek was a hike in the sand dunes. Once over the first ridge you could only see sand and most of that was in steep slopes down into fifty foot deep trenches. It was hard to get back up out of those trenches with the sand sliding under your feet faster than you could climb, and it was hot down there out of the wind. Mice and gophers that accidentally got into one never got out and their bones littered the hard pan at the bottom. The perfectly preserved and bleached skeletons were fascinating to boys and occasionally someone would find a beautiful flint arrowhead. We never found coyote skeletons. I guess they were smart enough not to get caught.

The game we never tired of was to scramble up to a crest and then throw ourselves back into the pit, rolling and flailing in the soft sand. The resistance kept you slowed down so no one ever got hurt.

One of Skipper's "things" was to lecture us on the power of mind over matter. You were hot? "It's all in your mind. Imagine yourself in the middle of a Saskatchewan Blizzard and you'll soon be shivering." You were thirsty? "Think of drowning out on the ocean and you soon wouldn't want water."

One hot July day Skipper brought me into a plot to teach an object lesson. He would take the troop well out into the sand hills for lunch but would "forget" to take the water. I would come behind with the water but stay out of sight. He gave us lots of practice stalking so we knew how to stay out of sight.

Lunch was dry sandwiches and of course by noon the boys were dying of thirst when Skipper dropped the bombshell that there was no water. He emptied the lunch pack to prove the point. The creek was an hour back to the north and the temperature was over 100 Fahrenheit.

PANIC!

Of course Skipper came on with the lecture about it being all in their minds. He sat there and ate his sandwich. The boys couldn't even put one in their mouths with their tongues all swollen up like that. Some wanted to head back fast. Others were on the verge of tears, knowing they were going to die. Skipper just smiled and finished his sandwich.

Then he gave three blasts on his whistle and I came over the top of the dune with the water bag.

It was a good object lesson. He said "OK guys, no water till you eat your sandwich. Water dilutes the saliva and slows down digestion." Miraculously, saliva came back into all the parched mouths and they ate their sandwiches. They didn't even drink all the water afterwards. You remember lessons like that.

Coyotes

One of my fondest memories of Beaver Creek is the coyotes. Scouts never saw them. Scouts are too noisy and no amount of persuasion can keep them quiet for more than thirty seconds. The one exception was Happy Hollow, which we will get to later.

The Creek was home to innumerable coyotes because of the wildlife centred there and because the area was not farmed. Nobody bothered trying to eradicate them from the creek and the sand hills. Some farmers, particularly of Eastern European origins, were actually afraid of coyotes because they sounded like wolves, and the European myths regarding wolves are ingrained deep in the psych.

A hungry coyote can be a risk to small, unattended children, but anyone over the age of six has nothing to fear. The coyotes at the creek were never hungry either.

What everyone who ever spent a night at the creek did hear was the coyotes howling at the moon. Actually they didn't need a moon to howl but a clear night with a full moon was a guarantee of a major chorus. There is little resemblance between a wolf howl and a coyote howl. Coyotes are higher pitched and more musical, with a lot of yipping in between the long drawn out yodels. It is music I never tired of hearing and is right up there with the loons and the Canada geese as a distinctive Canadian sound.

It was of course a given that all scouts imagined that they could howl like a coyote. We had contests to choose the best howler during daylight hours and then would wait for the nightly serenade to begin. When it would reach a pitch with many voices raised the best howler in the troop would get the signal and would lift his head and let go a howl at the moon. The result was always the same. Dead silence. No more coyote howls that night. Next camp a new howler would get to try his luck.

I know they howl to wolves in Algonquin Park and the wolves either answer them or perhaps just ignore them and keep howling anyway. Coyotes are smarter than that. They aren't going to fraternize with a species as unstable as human beings.

24ᵀᴴ OF MAY SWIM

"The 24th of May is the queen's birthday. If you don't give us a holiday we'll all run away." I don't know where this doggerel originated but we all used it anyway. As far as I know it has always been a holiday, but maybe way-back-when, people had to fight for it. In any case it marked the beginning of summer in Saskatoon and the first camp of the year at Beaver Creek.

Summer it may have been but ice always formed on the creek at night on that weekend. The winter ice was gone but when the sun went down it still froze. June, July, and August are the only normally frost free months in Saskatoon and the area has seen killing frost even in July and August. The first week in June is pretty shaky every year. Unfortunately, the Saskatoon berries bloom that week so they get frozen off about four years in five.

All the troops in Saskatoon usually converged on Beaver Creek for the 24th of May weekend. Major campfires were the rule for Saturday night but the ritual Sunday morning was something Skipper referred to as Kipper Wash. Undoubtedly a British term whose origin escapes me. Kipper Wash in the creek at six AM on the queens birthday consisted of skinny dipping and the first ones in had to literally break the ice. An eighth of an inch of new ice is cold and the pieces are sharp. The ritual was always accomplished with an incredible amount of screaming.

Of course pictures had to be taken by the Scouter, who was thereby relieved of participating in this rite of spring, but there was a problem. First of all everyone had to be in the water at the same time and gathered close enough for the camera to get them all in. And then we were all naked so everyone had to be deep enough to cover the essential parts. Scouts who couldn't make it on their own had to be submerged by their peers, who were not in a mood by this time to stop at the waist.

Inevitably there would occasionally be one kid with the forbidden parts above the water, and there is one famous cover photo on the scout magazine, "the leader", with a boy not quite deep enough in the water. It escaped the editors but many magnifying glasses established beyond doubt that the magazine had erred on the side of nudity.

November Swim

First Aid - Don't Leave Home Without It

One thing all scouts learn is first aid. Unfortunately it is an abstract subject for them. They know about band aids and sunburn cream from their mothers but serious injury can only be appreciated first hand. Also unfortunately, the same thing applies to a lot of leaders.

So first aid nights are a lot of fun. The kids can tie each other up in triangular bandages and make believe catastrophes, but it never actually sinks in. Bleeding - RED - rest, elevation, direct pressure. Hammer mnemonics like this often enough and they will remember; but will it mean anything when blood is spurting from someone like a garden hose (a severed artery is an impressive sight). The big problem is that no one believes they will ever have to use it and thankfully that is true for most of us.

All troops have a first aid kit. They don't always remember to take it.

I was one of those odd people who learned first aid well enough to get my St. Johns certificate. It therefore fell to me to be the official first aider for regional camps at Beaver Creek. The twelfth troop had an excellent first aid kit and Skipper always saw to it that it was kept up to date. There are advantages to military training.

One lovely summer day at a regional camp I was swimming with the guys when a panic stricken kid from a troop about a kilometre from us came running up yelling that Joe had chopped his arm with an axe and was bleeding to death. That doesn't do anything for the nerves. Fortunately I was a good runner so by the time I arrived with the first aid kit I could still function. Joe was unconscious in a small one room cabin at the headquarters site.

There was blood everywhere; the floor, the table, the walls, all over several adults and numerous boys. They had a tourniquet around his arm and the blood still gushed out of his wrist.

They had started by putting his hand in a pail of water. No reason for that but panic. The pail immediately turned red and Joe fainted. No one apparently remembered RED. REST - ELEVATION - DIRECT PRESSURE. No one believes that will work when they see so much blood.

I looked at the cut. It was a nice slice across his left wrist caused by a hatchet that had glanced off whatever he was chopping. The blood flowed steadily. Not arterial, thank God, or he'd have been dead before I got there.

I yelled for a triangular bandage and a sterile pad and started removing the tourniquet, over strong objections from the boy's Scouter who apparently only knew about tourniquets. RED. Joe had already taken care of R. He was completely at rest and fortunately didn't see most of what had gone on. E could wait a few seconds. I put the sterile pad over the cut, wrapped the triangular bandage around that and tied it tight but not enough to cut off the kid's circulation. Then I gave his hand to a scout standing there and told him to hold it up as high as he could and not let go till Joe was in the hospital.

The hospital was twenty minutes away by car at far too high a speed but the kid held Joe's hand high all the way. He had not lost nearly as much blood as the condition of the cabin seemed to indicate and was conscious before we loaded him into the car.

My point is that this was not a serious cut if it had been handled correctly when it happened. The doctor at Emergency complimented the first aid treatment but was curious about why everyone in the party had so much blood splattered over them. I don't think anyone explained. Joe actually had to have a transfusion because of blood loss. The correct application of RED at the start would have made it a minor incident.

I expect that troop focused on first aid for a while.

THE DISTRICT COMMISSIONER AND THE LEGION DINNER

Our District Commissioner in Saskatoon was an old British war veteran. He was probably only 60 but we boys thought of him as ancient. Someone out of the history books. At any rate, he was a member of the Canadian Legion and faithfully attended all of their functions. He didn't drink, so beer has nothing to do with this story.

The other happening that comes into this little drama is that in 1952 or thereabouts television had just arrived in Saskatoon. People were not quite sure what to do with it but it was obvious that you could now bring events like the Legion Dinner to everyone who owned a TV set. Thousands could now hear the after dinner political speeches. And that is what happened.

Believe it or not, the medium was so new that everyone with a TV set did watch the after dinner speeches. Only they never took place.

The head of the Legion got up to introduce the first speaker. The TV cameras zeroed in on his face, but he didn't look so good. A bit green about the gills. He said a few words and then abruptly sat down. The cameras faithfully followed and the viewers were all glued to the screen when he threw up on the table in front of him. A close up of someone throwing up is not something you see every day.

The camera operators were new at the game and they were slow to react. Finally they swung to the first speaker just in time for the viewing audience to watch him repeat the performance of the Legion head and then collapse forward into the mess.

In panic now the cameras panned the rest of the head table, recording each member following their leaders into the debacle. A sweep of the hall quickly confirmed the extent of the disaster as literally everyone who had eaten the potato salad succumbed to the salmonella which had become established during a night of less than adequate refrigeration.

The TV coverage had one good effect. The entire city knew immediately of the problem and medical people and ambulances converged on the Legion hall in record time, preventing the disaster from becoming a mass funeral.

One detail escaped notice. There was no record of who was at the function and no one thought to check. It seemed pretty obvious that everyone present was still there when the ambulances arrived.

The next day some of the scouts went down to headquarters to get some badges but found the building locked. On reporting this to our Scouter, he concluded that the Commissioner had been at the Legion dinner and was probably among the hundreds now in hospital. He would enquire.

The following day, no sign of the Commissioner had surfaced. He wasn't in any of the city hospitals. Skipper got a key to Scout Headquarters from somewhere so we could see if there was some clue there as to where he had gone. The first thing to hit us when the door opened was the stench. The Commissioner was lying on the floor in his two day old vomit just inside the door.

He was alive but just barely. It says something for the men that survived the First World War trenches that he lived and was back at his post two weeks later. He was as tough as old shoe leather.

His story was that he had been served first and had therefor become ill sooner than everyone else. Not wanting to upset the proceedings, he had discreetly left. Unfortunately the poison had affected his reasoning by this time and he had returned to Scout headquarters instead of seeking medical attention. He had managed to unlock the door and get inside before he collapsed. Unfortunately, the door was self locking, and nearly sealed his fate when it closed of its own volition.

The Cigarette Caper

I may have mentioned earlier that one of the scouters I had when the troop was new was a very sensitive guy. He was dismissed later, probably unjustly, on suspicion of being gay. At any rate he had this group of boys from the far East side of Saskatoon that was little more than a street gang. When we weren't in scout uniform (scouts actually wore uniforms in those days, short pants and all), we called ourselves the Bushwhackers. That was because we had a hut made out of willow fronds in the centre of a willow swamp where the ash grade crossed the 11th street slough.

It was called the ash grade because it was a causeway across the slough made from the cinders from Saskatoon's coal fired power station. One of the tests for toughness was to walk its whole length in your bare feet.

At any rate, our well meaning scouter had set himself the task of civilizing this bunch of rabble, and one of his objectives was to stamp out smoking. Now most of the boys smoked willow leaves. I think the effect came from the acetylsalicylic acid (aspirin) in the leaves. Who could afford cigarettes? A dime for the Saturday morning movie at the Ritz was the most any of us got for allowance.

I remember the night well. It was on the banks of the Saskatchewan and the moon was up. We had had our meeting outdoors, played a bunch of wide games and finished with a weaner roast. Scouter ran good meetings except for the end when he always gave us a little talk that no one understood, about how scouts should be. The one thing that was clear was that scouts should not be like us.

This particular night, when he had us quiet enough to be heard, he sat at the speakers place in the circle and hauled out a brand new pack of cigarettes, holding it up for all of us to see in the moonlight.

Dead silence. He finally had everyone's attention. I got a sinking feeling in my stomach (at the age of twelve I already had a stomach ulcer, I think because I really didn't fit the society I grew up in). I didn't smoke. Not tobacco and not willow leaves, but I knew my friends and in the presence of real tobacco they weren't boys, they were animals.

Well, they held on through the pitch about how tobacco was the devil's tool and as good scouts we sure didn't want to have any truck with the devil. He then opened the pack, shook the cigarettes out on the ground, said he wouldn't stay to see if we could resist temptation and turned and ran off into the night.

Pandemonium. Twenty four boys landed in a heap on the cigarettes, cursing and screaming and clawing. In the end, they were better scouts than I imagined. The ones with cigarettes, or pieces of cigarettes, actually shared them with the weak and the wounded and they were soon all laughing around the embers of the campfire, smoking those cigarettes down to the last butt and then piling the remains together so they could crouch over the little smudge pot and breath in the last fumes, cork tips and all.

As usual I stayed outside the circle of firelight and watched in fascination as my mates went through a ritual that I couldn't fathom. I couldn't stand tobacco smoke and still can't.   Scouter never came back and after a few minutes I went out looking for him. Once I was away from the fire and the noise I stopped and listened and soon I heard a sound that wasn't night sound. I zeroed in on it quietly and found scouter sitting in a little clearing, curled up with his head on his knees.

He was crying.

Happy Hollow Sex Education

After I inherited the Twelfth Troop at the age of eighteen, I continued to concentrate on camping, winter and summer. Camping is easy on the brain and on the discipline. A lot of the kids were only a year or two younger than me and we had been scouts together under an exceptional scouter. Discipline wasn't always easy indoors. I had one advantage. My kid brother was in the troop. Six years my junior, he was already bigger and stronger than me and had a penchant for exercising authority by brute force. I had an enforcer.

Just as an aside, one of the most successful patrols we had was led by what is now termed a nerd. A kid too tall for his age, gangly and uncoordinated and smart. Straight A's in school do not impress most scouts but John had my brother in his patrol. John did the thinking. Larry did the enforcing. It worked like a charm.

You don't need much of a program at camp. Most of the time is spent just surviving and the boys tend to listen because it amounts to self inflicted discomfort if you mess up (like leaving your food within reach of skunks or raccoons at night).

If chores run out before the next meal, there are all kinds of wide games you can play. You could try teaching them something but that is usually a miserable failure. You want to teach compass and map reading? Better make a game out of it. They only learn by getting lost. Boys aren't long on abstract thought and hypothetical situations.

Another aside here. In one compass game I set up two groups of boys arrived at a check point I was watching at the same time. They were in a race so they were in a hurry. They both set off at the same time, studiously ignoring each other, one group heading off about ten degrees West of the other. They should have been on the same course, with one group ahead by about two minutes. The group heading left was faster and had caught up.

As the two teams diverged, I saw the one on the right getting more and more nervous. They would stop and look at the other team and then argue. Finally they broke and just followed the other team, which of course was wrong. So they both lost the race. It's called having the courage of your convictions.

Happy Hollow no longer exists. The city has rolled over it, but at the time it was a spot on the North bank of the Saskatchewan just West of the city. It was a favourite picnic and day camp site because it was easily accessible. It had the river and trees and open spaces for whatever activity you could want. It also had an artesian well coming straight up from the potash beds far below. One mouthful of that bitter brew could cure any case of constipation within minutes.

So we were out for the day, and I had some new boys just up from cubs and completely green when it came to looking after themselves. One type of wide game requires stalking skills, and we decided to play one of these. Scouters love this type of game because it takes an hour or more and the object is to sneak around as quietly and invisibly as possible. Once under way, scouter can find a tree in the shade, lie down and have a quiet snooze.

Cubs can not play these games. Cubs operate on the verbal level, the louder the better. It's probably a survival instinct, intended to help adults keep track of these little kids who can get lost running around a tree.

So I was not expecting much of a peaceful afternoon, but I found my tree anyway and lay down to wait. Half an hour later I woke from a doze to realize that I hadn't heard a sound of any kind. Unusual for scouts. Unbelievable for cubs and the alarm bells went off. I jumped up and listened. Nothing. I woke my assistant who had also dozed off and got him to listen. Then we both got uneasy.

With no idea where they might have got to we went off in different directions to try to locate somebody. I had been reconnoitring for maybe ten minutes when my assistant came running up. He put his finger to his lips and motioned for me to follow. We crept up on a clearing in a dense grove of Manitoba Maples and he motioned me to keep down and quiet. I eased to the edge of the clearing and there in the middle was a blanket with some vigorous movement going on beneath it. He pointed silently across the clearing and I soon picked out the heads of several scouts, cubs among them, silently watching the spectacle.

I looked at my assistant. He shrugged and motioned a retreat. What could you do? Blow the whistle and bring all those boys running across the clearing?

We went back to our tree and waited. We waited a long time. The game finally ended and the boys returned chattering excitedly among themselves. No one mentioned what they had been doing but it was obvious that they had learned their stalking lessons well.

The Bottle Drive

One of the everlasting problems for scouts, or any other organization for that matter, is money. Before recycling there were two labour intensive but very lucrative means of raising money; paper drives and bottle drives.

One thing scout groups have is lots of slave labour, both kids and parents. Parents have weak backs but strong cars and trucks. Traditionally, areas were divided up among the established troops and each troop worked its own area. To step over your border was to invite a gang war. And with good reason. A good paper drive could fund all the camping equipment you needed or send your contingent to a jamboree; maybe even a world jamboree in some far away place.

I was not very old when the great Saskatoon bottle drive happened. Maybe still a cub. I don't remember. Probably a cub because they haven't figured out yet that you can get by with less than complete dedication to whatever is going on. I remember the endless piles of bottles very well. Saskatoon was a prairie city and a lot of beer went down the hatch in the hot summers. It wasn't easy to return the bottles either. You had to take them downtown and then they were only two cents apiece. Most of my spending money as a kid came from collecting bottles from the roadsides (my parents were tea-totalers) and hauling them down to the bottle man on my bike.

Unfortunately, organizations like scouts also have regional councils which are also always short of cash. This particular year, Saskatoon's regional council got a flash of inspiration. Since the individual troops all seemed to do so well on bottles, why not get them all to have a drive on the same day? Council would provide a couple of trucks and a central storage site, do all the paper work, divide up the take among the troops and of course skim off enough cream to run regional council for the next year.

What they didn't have was any experience on the front line.

The day dawned bright and clear and hot. All summer days dawn bright and clear and hot in Saskatoon. There was no premonition of disaster as each troop did what it always did. Kids and parents gathered at the scout hall, got a map with their area marked out and away we went. Each little unit took about two hours to cover their route and bring the bottles back to their own scout hall.

It was near the end of this phase that something started to go wrong. The trucks from headquarters didn't show up to cart the bottles away and the troops had made no arrangements other than piling them on the side walk in front of their hall, usually a church and this was Saturday night.

Poor Regional Council. They had not bothered to find out just how many bottles went in to a regular bottle drive. On top of that, this one had been advertised, so the whole city was prepared to get rid of their bottles. Some areas had never been collected before.

Bottles started to arrive in a river that soon turned into an avalanche. They had one single garage to store them in. The normal bottle return could handle at most the take from one troop on any given day. It was just a shack run by an old alcoholic who drained the drops from each bottle he bought and managed to stay more or less drunk in that manner.

Of course the garage overflowed within the first hour and bottles spilled into the street. As panic mounted bottles were dumped rather than lifted carefully off. The collection area became a field of broken glass and any hope of sorting the soft drink bottles from the beer bottles quickly died.

Soon the street was blocked which was against city bylaws. No one had got a permit to block the street. The constabulary arrived and said "here, here now - what is going on?" Soon other city officials arrived with no advice other than that something would have to be done. Regional council members were nearing physical and mental collapse (they thought "be prepared" was a motto only for scouts).

The solution did not arrive until the next day. Sunday. The bottles would have to be gone by start of work Monday and there was no way to dispose of that many by the usual method. There was no available storage space and no volunteers left capable of moving them even if a space had been found. Regional Council hired a trucking firm with front end loaders at overtime rates to haul all the bottles off to the municipal dump.

And so ended the Great Saskatoon Bottle Drive.

The Hoop Dance

The Scouter I grew up under was an ex-military physical fitness instructor. He was also a nut on Canadian Indian lore. The troop made a teepee, authentic down to the nineteen tamarack poles that went with it. The entire troop could hold a meeting in it if it rained at camp. A meeting with a campfire yet. The designs painted on the thousand square feet of canvas were authentic reproductions of prairie Indian motifs. The long, thin poles for the teepee were cut at Christopher lake, before increasing population stopped that sort of thing.

The teepee wasn't the only thing. Every scout had to make his own indian costume. Loin cloth, leggings, moccasins, roche. A roche is a head gear made from the hair of a horse's tail and died red. It looks like a brush four or five inches deep and two inches wide that goes from the centre of the forehead to the nape of the neck and is held in place by a head band. All of this had to be beaded with authentic indian designs by the boys own hand. No help from mother. Scout's honour.

Author at age 16 with home made Roches

It's evident that we didn't have television in those days.

Skipper was the chief of course. The only one who had the big feathered headdress. We were an impressive sight at summer camp at Christopher lake, where we had "indian days" during which we spent the whole time in our indian outfits and ended the day with a pow wow around a campfire in front of the teepee, authentic indian dances and the works. It was the dances that brought out the physical fitness instructor in Skipper. The indians from the local reservation came to watch as well as all the cottagers.

Needless to say, the troop gained some attention at home for all of this. The teepee was often set up on the church lawn so we could practice and people would stop and talk to the Big Chief, who would talk to anyone at any length on his pet subject.

And that brings us around to the "Indian Night" that Skipper got us into. Interest had grown to the point where someone suggested that we should put on a pow wow for the church congregation. It was to be inside because it was winter but the church wasn't big enough. Skipper reserved what we thought was an immense hall, but it still wasn't big enough to put the teepee up. With the poles it rose about 25 feet with about 350 square feet of floor space.

A certain amount of hype went into the publicity. Skipper was a born showman and that's where the hoop dance comes in. Now the hoop dance is a very athletic dance. It involves a dancer bouncing around with a thing like a hula hoop, imitating various animals and birds. It is becoming well known today because indian culture showplaces are springing up here and there as tourist attractions and they are quite popular. Of course they use much more complicated versions of the dance than we ever attempted.

We only had one scout who was flexible enough and smart enough to remember all the contortions for this dance. Suffice it to say that he eventually became wrestler of the year four times at the University of Saskatchewan, and he was labelled as the star attraction.

Well, we practised and practised and even we thought we were pretty good. Not much nerves because we knew only parents would come anyway and we had danced for them before. Little did we know.

Author with drum, Elgin with hoop

The hall had a separate room for us to dress in and we didn't see the audience until we entered the hall. Our lead dancer went first, with Skipper bringing up the rear. He stopped dead at the door. There was no room to get through to the dance circle. Slowly the crowd parted and we squeezed through people we didn't know. These were not just parents and our knees started to shake a bit. Then came the circle.

It was surrounded to the last inch by girls and we twenty five boys were essentially naked except for loin cloths and moccasins. Skipper sailed in with his nose in the air and an enigmatic expression befitting a chief of the tribe. At a signal from him the dance began. We got a lot of applause after all the dances and were getting used to being on stage. Of course it ended with the hoop dance with only our star in the centre and me beating a drum. The rest of us got to squat at the back and watch. We watched the girls watching the hoop dancer and it was a revelation.

Girls liked us. Or at least him. When he stopped they screamed and yelled and whistled. We would have run but there was nowhere to hide as all these people broke ranks and cornered us to talk about our show. It's not an easy thing for young teenage boys nearly stark naked to make conversation with a lot of excited but fully clothed girls we didn't even know.

The next meeting was devoted to lectures about the dangers of temptation and what the proper attitude towards the opposite sex should be.

Archery in the Church Hall

Skipper introduced us to a lot of things. He was also a fencing instructor and obtained some old foils and masks. We tried, but the stance required was more than boys our age could handle. It looks so easy when real swordsmen do it but holding a half squat and zooming back and forth like a demented crab soon dampens the enthusiasm.

Another thing he got us into was archery. Now archery is not an easy thing to practice without the proper facilities. You should really have a large field with a fence to keep innocent bystanders out of the line of fire. You should have targets that stop the arrows. None of these problems deterred Skipper.

I must put a word in here for the church I grew up in. Grace United in Saskatoon. I have never run across another church that would put up with the things we did in their hall, which was just the basement under the main sanctuary. We cut out the canvas for the teepee down there and we painted it down there. The room must have been 75 feet long and had rooms all around the periphery. It also had curtains that could be pulled across one end to make a stage for plays. That's what made the archery possible. Anyone out there know of another church that would let a gang of boys shoot bows and arrows in their hall with only a light curtain for a backstop?

Skipper knew a lot about ballistics and one of the things he knew was that a silk stocking could stop a bullet. Hang a silk stocking from a clothes line and fire a rifle at it and the bullet will wrap itself in the material which then stretches and deflects the bullet into an arc which dissipates the energy and the bullet stops. Of course the stocking has to be hanging with one end free. The same stocking on your leg won't even slow a bullet down. Neither will your leg.

So, Skipper reasoned, the curtain at the end of the hall, hanging from the ceiling with the other end free should stop an arrow with no trouble. A demonstration was arranged and since I was the troop leader I got to shoot the arrow. It was a 25 lb. target bow so it didn't pack a huge wallop but you still wouldn't want to get hit. An arrow is much heavier than a bullet so even if it is a lot slower it carries a similar kinetic energy. In other words it's just as hard to stop. We need not have worried. Skipper knew his ballistics. The arrow went pouf into the curtain which hardly moved, and then fell quietly to the floor.

The church hall committee was happy and we proceeded to learn archery. We got several bows and a few blunt end arrows. No need of razor sharp hunting arrows for basic practice. After the first few skinned fingers and wrists from bow string burns we gradually collected wrist guards and finger tabs too. We had to make our own targets which simply got pinned to the curtain and after a month or so most of the boys could hit the curtain if not the target. There were a few scratches on the floor and ceiling from arrows that went astray but nothing that alarmed the church hall committee enough to call a halt.

Archery practice had another spin off. Somehow Skipper always managed to involve girls in the activities somewhere. Thinking about it much later I suspect that girls were a part of what he considered the proper training of the well rounded scout.

We had CGIT at Grace church. Canadian Girls In Training. They weren't Girl Guides but a similar program run by the United Church for well behaved girls. At any rate, once we were good enough not to embarrass ourselves, Skipper invited the CGIT to come down and get archery lessons.

Now this is really a touchy thing for a bunch of 14 to 16 year old boys to do. It quickly became evident after the first awkward advances (how come boys always have to be awkward when girls are around) that the best way to demonstrate was to place the bow and arrow in the girls hands and then take up a position behind her, wrap your arms around far enough to place your hands over hers and then carefully aim and draw. This entailed getting two heads close enough together to see the same arrow and target. It was amazing how many times this had to be repeated before the girls got the idea.

I'm sure it had nothing to do with it but I eventually married one of our archery pupils.

So life on the range was good. Unfortunately there is always someone in human endeavours not happy to let well enough alone. Brian was such a one and Brian had noticed that the curtain did not quite meet in the middle. It was only a half inch gap which says something for his accuracy with a bow. He hoped to claim bad aim but his record and the fact that the target was several feet from the gap in the curtains played against him.

The girls were in for their lessons and Brian always liked to find some way to show off. They were no longer impressed just by hitting the target since they could all do that too. So Brian notched an arrow, took careful aim and sent the arrow through the gap in the curtains without so much as a ripple. Behind the curtains was the piano and the chord he struck reverberated through the hall and up into the church.

It didn't do any real damage to the instrument but the oak of a piano is not a loose curtain. The arrow went through a couple of inches and stuck. There was no getting it out without a chisel and the noise had attracted the minister from the church office upstairs. When he arrived the evidence was still stuck solidly in the centre of the piano with the culprit frantically trying to extract it. So ended archery practice in the church hall.

Gilwell Training and the Wood Badge Beads

To be a competent scouter you need some training. Apart from the years I spent with Skipper, there was also formal training, some correspondence which consisted of reading books and mailing in exam papers, and some just putting in your time as an assistant.

Then there was the Wood Badge. Originally this was a ten day or so camp for aspiring troop scouters held at the official scout campground set up by Lord Baden-Powell at Gilwell in England. Hence the name Gilwell training. As the movement spread however, these training camps were conducted throughout the world. When I was eighteen, I stopped off at the Little Red River near Prince Albert, on the way home from our summer camp at Christopher Lake, for my Wood Badge course.

I was the youngest trainee there and my ten days were complicated somewhat by the fact that I had met a Prince Albert girl at Christopher Lake who came out to the camp at every opportunity to watch what we were doing. I was madly in love which does nothing for eighteen year old mental capacity. I thought she came to see me, although we had no chance to actually talk to each other. Things were run very formally in those days and boys and girls were not supposed to mix. She, on the other hand was only mildly interested in me. She had been impressed by our indian day at Christopher Lake and wanted to become a cub leader. She made it. I didn't.

The course was conducted like a scout camp and all we scouters were divided into patrols, with patrol leaders and seconds, just like a scout troop. Headquarters was staffed by people from head office in Ottawa. Of course we all thought these guys were the gurus of scouting. It became evident over the ten days that they didn't know much more about it than we did but everyone tried valiantly to bring it off, which is really all that happens at any scout camp anyway. They were long on theory and I was long on practice. They were old guys and I was a kid. All this made for a bit of tension at times.

Another thing was that they were still back in the old army tradition. Lots of marching and protocol, flag ceremonies and campsite inspections. Pots that had been used to cook over open fires were very big on the agenda. They didn't have to be cleaned. They had to be polished inside and out. Now cleanliness is next to godliness but I knew how long a bunch of boys would stay in a troop where an hour each morning was spent polishing pots for a bunch of old guys to inspect.

A lot of this had to do with using up time so you didn't run out of program ideas. Actually there is no problem with program at camp. If you are tired, give the kids some free time. they will always find something amusing to do (of which more in another chapter).

I don't wish to run down Gilwell training. A lot of good things came out of those ten days, not least of which was getting to know the other guys in my patrol. We had a young RCMP officer who was stationed in a backwoods community with a youth problem. He had been told to start a scout troop as one solution. We had a Mormon a year older than me, married with a kid. His church ran everything and he had been assigned the job of being the local scouter. He never questioned the assignment. We had an honest to god cowboy from Alberta who had never been a scout and knew he had missed something. He was born on a horse and his legs were so bowed he walked just like they did in the old movies. He also played a guitar and sang songs no one had ever heard of. Songs the cows liked.

The mountie was married, and in those days that was an accomplishment for a mountie. He had been on some assignment for a month before he came to the Gilwell camp and had not even got a visit home before coming. His favourite theme after lights out was to complain about the injustice of life. According to him, young married people should make love every night, but if you were separated for a month you couldn't save it up and make love thirty times in one night. Just once and then all those missed nights were gone and no way to get them back.

The mormon thought this was a pretty strange attitude for a mountie. He had married when the church had picked a mate for him. The church decided what he did, and when, and he thought that's the way it should be. Other than that he seemed just like me and we were friends.

The cowboy had some personal problems he never talked about. Maybe he had never had anyone but cows to talk to. For those who had not come up through scouts, there was an investiture at the last campfire, where they swore allegiance to the queen and received their tenderfoot badge. The cowboy cried and that night went off by himself and played his guitar long into the night. Nobody interfered.

Campfire was the most painful part of the course. Each patrol had to plan campfire program one of the nights. Now popular belief is that campfire is the highlight of every scout camp. That is a myth as false as the hollywood indian. In fact no one can ever think of anything they really want to do at a campfire and that goes for scouters as well as scouts. Scouts have to be lined up and driven to campfire. There they are made to sing songs they don't want to sing and perform skits they don't want to perform and applaud others they don't even want to watch. When it's over they are expected to go to bed and shut up (which they never, ever do).

What scouts want to do is sit around their own little fire at their own tent and talk about whatever interests them long into the night. Usually sex. And they don't want adults around. Think about that and you will recognize exactly what adults want to do at camp. Sit in the cool of the evening around a little fire and shoot the breeze.

Girls are different. If you want a good scout type campfire with songs and skits and shrieking laughter and a really fun time, then go out with a bunch of girls. That's their thing.

This tale does not have a happy ending for me. The reward for surviving Gilwell training is to receive the Wood Badge and Beads. These are two carved wooden beads on a leather thong worn with pride by scouters and recognized as a symbol of someone who has paid his dues and knows what it is all about. For some reason they are not handed out at the last campfire. They come with a certificate from national headquarters in Ottawa to the District Commissioner of your area. Usually there is a local ceremony where they are presented.

Mine never came.

Skipper waited a respectful period and then took me aside one night and explained that one failure was not the end of the world. That I should not take it too hard since I was very young. He thought that might be the reason that they passed me by. I was wounded worse than I was willing to admit. They never even sent me a rejection note saying why I was not good enough.

Three years later I was working for a fire insurance company in Saskatoon and one day the manager of my branch called me in. He had been the District Commissioner the year I went to Gilwell camp. He said "are you in scouts?" I said that I was the scouter of the twelfth Saskatoon troop. He said "I guess these must be yours then. I was cleaning out some old files and found them in the bottom of a drawer."

My Wood Badge and Beads. I kept them but I never wore them

CHRISTOPHER LAKE

As you will have gathered by now, Christopher Lake was our usual summer camp. It is North of Prince Albert on the way to Waskesiu, a small lake as lakes go in that area but it had everything you could ask for in a camp. There was a little store where you could get fresh meat and other perishables, so you didn't have to live on bulgur like you would on a canoe trip. There wasn't much else to distract the boys, except a few girls from the cottages and a girl guide camp across the lake. Well, you can't have everything.

The girl guide camp had permanent buildings. Girls were not expected to sleep in tents in those days. Unfortunately we had the usual complement of budding thugs in our troop and some of them took it into their heads to attack the girls camp. Of course there was no one there at the time.

I won't go into details but they did a pretty good job of messing it up but, as often happens to the bad guys, they got caught and suddenly it wasn't a joke any more. Skipper was not an army sergeant for nothing and he did not intend that we get expelled from our camp for disturbing the peace. It took a couple of days out of our intended program but the culprits cleaned up the girls camp. They polished it up. They repaired everything including stuff they hadn't broken. They got busted back to tenderfoot and had to earn all their badges over again from the start.

That was the only bad thing that ever happened at Christopher Lake, but each camp had its share of incidents, most of them funny. Like the patrol that was winning all the point contests.

The patrol leader eventually became a vice-president of Ontario Hydro so he obviously had some smarts. One of the competitions was the first patrol to finish breakfast and clean up well enough to pass inspection each morning. This year it rained at the lake nearly the whole week and getting a fire started in the morning was a daunting task. This patrol not only got its fire going first every morning but they greeted Skipper in his sleeping bag daily with a cup of coffee before anyone else had their fire started. After the first two days no one even tried to compete.

Until about day five. I was troop leader by this time and shared headquarters tent with Skipper. This was a mixed privilege because he chain smoked and I hated cigarette smoke. At any rate we were lying awake this morning listening to the sounds of camp beginning to stir when there was suddenly screaming and running feet going past the tent. We scrambled out just in time to see our prize patrol diving into the lake fully clothed. They submerged and didn't come up.

Of course they eventually did but by this time we were down at the beach to find out what had happened. Yellow jackets is what had happened. Wasps that is. A whole very angry nest of them had inflicted a few dozen stings on our prize patrol.

Now this was a bit strange at six o'clock in the morning, when all good wasps should have still been asleep. And why just one patrol? It took a bit of persuasion but finally the truth came out. On the first day while exploring the bush near camp they had come across a derelict tractor. Playing about this antique machine they had discovered that there was still some gas in the tank and they were able to drain some of it out.

Now our clever patrol leader realized right away that a little gas would make the job of starting the fire in the morning a lot easier, and that worked wonders until the fifth day, when they could coax no more gas out of the old wreck.

A solution occurred to our future engineer. If they could roll the tractor a few feet it would change the slope of the tank and a few more drops might be obtained. They got it into neutral and each boy put his shoulder to a spoke of each wheel. One! two! three! heave! And it moved. Once more now. One! two! three! heave! The tractor rolled forward several feet, and that's when the wasps struck.

They had a very large nest in one of the wheel hubs that was not easily visible. It was early morning and they were all at home.

Of course the patrol lost all its points for being the best fire lighters. We would have left it at that but the other patrols insisted on a further penalty for cheating. We made it as light as we could get away with. They had suffered enough.

One of the goons from the girl guide camp affair was an incorrigible. Some people are like that. They never seem to learn from mistakes. This particular boy also took to hacking at anything within reach with an axe. He was not a first class scout and did not have axe privileges. Finally in exasperation Skipper handed him a hatchet and said OK, if you want to chop, we'll find something for you to chop.

Now camp was surrounded with pine forest. It has probably been clear cut by this time but then the trees seemed endless and no one thought anything about conserving them. We went back in about fifty yards and found a tall pine about two feet in diameter. We watched while the miscreant cleared an area around the tree and then demonstrated that he could swing the small axe in the proper manner. Skipper told him to chop away until he couldn't chop any more, then to rest and chop away some more.

We went back to our program. Hour after hour we could hear the slow chopping coming from the bush so we knew he was still at it. We were just finishing lunch, listening to the distant chop, chop, chop and discussing whether to go in and relieve him of his punishment. Then a loud crack split the air. Conversation froze. Chop, chop, CRACK!

We jumped and ran for the tree but too late. With a thundering roar it came down in the forest and then all was still. When we got there our culprit was standing, sweat stained and haggard of face with one foot on the fallen giant. It had not occurred to us that he could even hurt the tree with that little hatchet, let alone fell it.

Skipper was never at a loss in any situation. He didn't want to just waste this tree we had unwittingly assassinated and he saw an opportunity to teach some engineering as well as axeman ship. We had big axes too and anyone wanting to pass their axeman ship took to the tree with the big axe and soon had it cut into four ten foot sections.

Now a green tree is incredibly heavy, but with skilful use of ropes and the hauling power of twenty five boys you can move incredible weights. You apply a timber hitch to both ends of a log, wrap the rope around it several times and then put the boys in man harness and yell pull. The log rolls.

Once the boys had the idea we left them to it and late in the afternoon our campfire circle had four logs around it for sitting on. Of course Skipper invited the cottagers to the pow wow that evening and they got to sit on them. He let them believe we had done all that just for their convenience.

The morning coffee had another funny twist. As I mentioned, Skipper chain smoked. He did that to the day he died at ninety eight. He was also very particular about his coffee. The coffee grounds were floated on top of the water and just as the first rolling boil sucked them under the pot was snatched from the flames. A pinch of salt was then added and it was served boiling hot.

One day my brother, who was six years younger than me, told me Skipper couldn't taste anything because of his smoking. I said he couldn't know that and he said he could. I said don't be silly and he said "bet on it".

Now one thing I learned the hard way is that you don't bet with my brother. But I did. He said OK, I make Skippers coffee every morning because he likes the way I make it. Come tomorrow morning and watch. When I came the next morning, the coffee pot was already boiling and had been for some time. It had not been yanked off the fire at the first rolling boil. When Larry saw that I had taken that in, he took it off the fire and put in a full teaspoon of salt. He stirred that up and took it to Skipper who was still in his sleeping bag. What I heard was "ah, that hits the spot. Nothing like a cup of coffee in the morning made the way I taught you. You're a good cook Larry."

Aborted Moves

THE LOG CABIN AT SPY HILL

My father was born in the dying years of the 19th century on lake Talon near North Bay, in the middle of a canoe trip heading West. He was the youngest of many brothers and sisters and the family was heading for Edson Alberta, where they ran a stopping place for the pioneers heading for Peace River homesteads. They arrived at their chosen spot which was nothing but unbroken forest, cut logs and built the stopping place beside the wagon trail a days drive north of Edson.

They had come from farming stock in the Westmeath area near Cobden, Ontario. Logging and farming was what they knew. Horses and cattle went along with the general picture. And hunting, of course. They were meat hunters and the idea of killing something for sport would have been incomprehensible to them. It was hard work that you did in order to eat.

I had a slingshot a soon as I could pull one, and a 22 rifle as soon as it was legal. My dad had one rule. Shoot whatever you want but you eat what you shoot. That does limit your killer instinct. It didn't apply to crows and gophers, which were considered mortal enemies of farmers, but certainly applied to black birds and any other innocuous species. Black birds taste pretty good actually but there's not much meat on them.

All this to explain what happened when I was in my late teens in Saskatoon. My dad had over the years ended up working for the Dominion Forage Crops Laboratories in Saskatoon as a greenhouse foreman. Now this was a secure job through the great depression but it paid subsistence wages and the pension that went with it would not keep a gopher going in post war Saskatoon.

Consequently, as the forced retirement age of 65 approached, dad was casting around frantically for some means of providing for his family when the end came. To go on "the dole" was not an option. He came from a line of people who would starve before accepting charity. Social welfare in those days was proof that you had failed to make the grade as a human being.

What he looked for was what he knew from his early days. Logging and farming. He had two strong sons and his vision was that we could get a woodlot concession up north, get a team of horses and some cows and chickens and pigs and go back to the pioneering life.

Now, he didn't have any options, but he also didn't take into account that his kids, two boys and two girls, had been raised in the city and didn't have a clue about any of this. He also did not realize that the days of the pioneer were gone and that it was no longer possible to hack a farm out of the bush by muscle power alone and survive. My older sister was old enough to opt out and that's what she did, so there were five of us.

What dad found was a place near Spy Hill, Saskatchewan that was for sale and apparently had a house and was near a logging area with woodlot concessions available. He found this in a real estate add and put in a bid. Fortunately the bid didn't commit him to any great penalty if he reneged.

On an August weekend we all piled into our 1926 Chevy and headed for Spy Hill to see our new home for the first time. At a top speed of 35 miles per hour it was a long trip and when we left the main road to Prince Albert we started to get into bush. Not forest. Bush. There may have been real logging there at one time but the big trees that dad remembered were long gone.

We eventually found the place. It had no yard to speak of and was just a one room log cabin. A young woman came out carrying a baby. They weren't tenants, they were just squatters, and they knew the place had been sold. She went and found her husband while we had a look around.

My brother and I never thought anything about it but my mother was going into shock. Our house on the outskirts of Saskatoon wasn't much but it did have electricity and four bedrooms (parents, girls, boys and grandparents), small mind you but still bedrooms.

The husband finally came out of the bush and started to say they would be gone by the time we wanted to move in. It was pretty obvious that he didn't know where they would be gone to and my dad said "whoa, wait a minute. You people just stay put. I don't think this is going to work out." I still remember the relief on the woman's face. She didn't break into tears. People that live on the verge like that don't cry easily, but it was obvious she had just heard a death sentence lifted.

We talked a while about the state of the forest and confirmed that a woodlot was no longer good for anything but cutting firewood for your own survival. Then we all got into our car and headed back to Saskatoon. Our poor little house looked like a mansion when we pulled in.

The Feeder Operation

A feeder operation is the business of buying the calves, usually unwanted ones from dairy operations, feeding them for six months or so and then selling them for beef. Dairy calves are not normally the best of beef cattle but they are good enough for the hamburger trade and one can make a profit if the prices don't do you in. You buy small calves in the spring at the going price per pound and they gain weight all summer out in the fields or in a feeder pen and then you sell them in the fall, hopefully for the same price per pound. If you can't sell them in the fall for a profit you can try feeding them all winter, hoping the price will go up by spring. Feeding in the winter is expensive and labour intensive so it is a risky business.

After the aborted try at logging at Spy Hill my dad decided to try a feeder operation. He knew what he was doing because his years as a greenhouse foreman for the Dominion Forage Crops Laboratories in Saskatoon had given him access to the latest in farm management thinking. He had one problem. The theories on investing in farming said you should have a dollar reserve for every dollar invested. That is so you can survive if the first year turns out bad, a very common occurrence in farming.

Well, dad didn't have that option. With the small house which had built up some equity, and cashing in the pension he had built up over the years, he had just enough to put a down payment on a section of land about fifteen miles West of Saskatoon. On top of that, we bought a cow, two little pigs, an antique John Deer tractor, an unmatched team of horses and thirty five head of young calves. The calves were bought for 35 cents a pound, an extremely high price at that time, but the feeder business was booming and the banks had no qualms about lending money to anyone going into that business.

The farm belonged to an old couple who were no longer working it. A lot had gone back to bush and the rest to prairie grass. It was all small rolling hills, poplar bluffs, small meadows and two sandy fields that could grow wheat or oats if it rained. That "if" is a big word in Saskatchewan.

Now all that grass was certainly sufficient to feed those calves for the first year without us doing anything, so things looked pretty good. We just turned them loose and let them graze, every pound they put on theoretically adding thirty-five cents to our pockets.

We used the horses to run a small hay mower which cut enough hay to feed the milk cow over the winter. The John Deer had a cracked head so every morning one cylinder was full of water. We had to remove the spark plug and start it on the other cylinder, whereupon a jet of water shot from the other cylinder hard enough to go through a two inch plank. You didn't want to be in the line of fire. We would then stop the tractor, put the spark plug back in and start it again fast so water would not fill the cylinder again before we got it going. It started with a hand crank which I never did get strong enough to use. Dad or my kid brother had to start it for me.

We planted wheat in the two fields but it wasn't easy. They grew grass all right but they were mostly sand and the tractor regularly got stuck in pockets of pure sand. You then had to unhitch the machinery you were pulling, attach a long enough chain to get the tractor on firm ground, pull out your plough or harrow or seeder or whatever and hook everything up again. If you stalled those old tractors it meant cranking them by hand, which could easily result in a broken arm if they back fired. The farm boys that had been raised with them had arms like a horses hind leg and could spin those cranks like toys. We had been raised in the city and for us it was an ordeal, so stalling the tractor was something you quickly learned not to do.

The summer went on as summers do in Saskatchewan, hot and dry, but with the backlog of grass, our beef was putting on weight at a satisfying rate. But then disaster struck. Foot and mouth disease hit Saskatchewan.

Maybe you don't know about foot and mouth disease. It comes from Europe, where they have learned to live with it. It does the cattle little harm, like flu in human beings. But they get a fever for a few weeks in the summer, they stop eating and THEY LOSE WEIGHT. They lose weight at 35 cents a pound and there goes your profit.

Now very few farms contracted foot and mouth disease and that brings up another idiosyncrasy of farm life. Those that got the disease were saved. Those that didn't were ruined. Read that again if you thought it was a misprint. The reason is simple if you know how governments work. The main customer for Canadian farm products is the United States. At the first hint of foot and mouth they close the border. No market.

Now the Canadian government can't let this situation go on so they act. They have to convince the Americans that they have the disease under control. No. More than that. Eradicated!

The solution is simple. Every time the disease is detected on a farm, government agents come in, shoot all the cattle on the place, dig a big hole and bury them and pay the farmer for them. The farmer smiles as he accepts the cheque and starts over.

But most farms didn't get the disease, ours among them. One day a calf came in from the field, its head hanging, lower lip drooping and drooling saliva. We called the vet, praying that it was foot and mouth. It wasn't. She had cut her lip on barbed wire.

Why were we so sad? Well, the Americans were not going to open up their border until there was no shadow of a suspicion of foot and mouth left in Canada. That was going to take a couple of years. In the meantime, no one could sell their cattle. No sale, no mortgage payments. We had no reserve to fall back on and the banks only wanted their money.

We had bought the calves for 35 cents a pound. We sold them for 5 cents a pound after feeding them for six months. We sold what hay we could harvest and then sold the horses. We couldn't sell the wheat because the government allowed only a small percentage quota, so we fed it to the two pigs and one small beef that we kept back to have something to eat. We couldn't sell the tractor so we gave it to a neighbour that was worse off than us. It was the first tractor he had ever owned.

When it was all gone and the banks had foreclosed, we were even. We didn't owe anything and we didn't own anything. I went back to Saskatoon to work for the post office sorting mail. My brother got on with a sheet metal worker. My dad took my mother and young sister to Edmonton, where an old friend from the laboratories got him a job as a janitor.

And so ended the feeder operation. As Robbie Burns said, the best laid plans gang aft aglay.

The Red Tailed Hawk

The Red Tailed Hawk is a magnificent bird common across the flat lands of Canada. Farmers used to shoot them when chickens roamed freely in the farm yards, before the days of the egg factories and automated broiler operations. It was hardly the fault of the hawks. They were here first and one of their natural food sources was wild chickens. The farm yards with big chickens that couldn't even fly were too much of a temptation. Even at that, their main diet was mice and gophers, so when the hawks got shot out the farmers had to resort to poisoning the other pests, which did in a lot of dogs and cats as well. The same rationale was used on coyotes and maybe still is. The results are the same too.

The Red Tail is bigger than the average chicken and spends most of its day gliding in lazy circles almost out of sight in the blue prairie sky. It's not often that you can see them up close. Except when they nest. Then they have to come down to earth, or at least as close as the top of the tallest poplar tree they can find.

I collected birds eggs as a hobby when I was a kid but the Red Tail was one I never got. I'm not afraid of height, but a limbless poplar 80 feet high is not your average climbing tree. Particularly with a bird that is not afraid to dive bomb you while you climb.

There is one day when they are vulnerable. When the young bird first leaves the nest it does so in its first attempt to fly. The flight ends in an exhausted glide to the ground, where the bird has to stay until it is rested enough to get into the air on its own. This takes about a full day with many aborted attempts to get into the air. During this time its only defence is the dive bombing attacks of the parents on anything that comes near.

A chicken caught by a Red Tail will be found to have eight holes drilled deep into it by the eight, two inch long talons the hawk possesses. It dies instantly. I have never seen holes like this in a boy but who wants to take the chance?

One of the memorable episodes from the feeder operation started the day my young brother found a Red Tail that had just left the nest. This was a real diversion from the daily routine and away we went to get a look. I was twenty three at the time and my brother was seventeen, so we were old enough to brave the attacks of the parent hawks and young enough to be sufficiently stupid to do it.

The hawk could fly about fifty meters before falling back to the ground exhausted. The time it took us to run that far while dodging the attacks of the parents was enough for it to catch its breath and fly another fifty meters. It took a while but we finally ended up at the house carrying a full grown and rather angry hawk. I suppose an expert could tell whether it was male or female but we never knew. The parents gave up once we had the bird captive. Wild animals are fatalists and know when to quit.

Dad was not too pleased and suggested we let the bird go, now that we had seen it up close. Larry was not about to do that without a fight. He wanted to show his friends first and that meant keeping it until the weekend. Dad finally relented but said "OK, but you make a perch about six feet high and tie a rope to its leg long enough that it can get to the ground and back up to the perch. Maybe the parents will come and feed it, but if they don't, then you have to keep it stuffed with mice until you let it go."

Hey! No problem. If our farm had one thing it was mice. Our big black tom cat continuously ate them till he threw up and then started over again.

Well, the parents did not come to feed it. Maybe we tethered it too close to the house. So after supper we started to hunt mice. Even with mice running everywhere, that is not as easy as it might seem. We also took to shooting sparrows with the twenty-two until Dad noted how much it was going to cost to feed it that way. It never filled up. That hawk could eat its weight in mice and sparrows every day.

About the end of the second day we were ready to call it quits when a miracle occurred. The hawk suddenly dropped from its perch and came up with a mouse all by itself. It could hunt! Now the small field by the house where we had it tethered was overrun by mice. Larry's friends had seen the hawk and since it could fend for itself it was time to release it. It was tame by this time and never bit the hands that fed it, so it sat quietly while we undid the rope. We backed off and watched but it just sat there. Then it flew twenty metres and pounced, coming up with another mouse. It flew back to the perch and happily ate its prey. It was homed to the perch!

Dad said "fine, the hawk can take care of itself. Take the perch down and let it get on with its life". So we did. The hawk (we never called it anything but hawk) flew to the top of the barn and took up its new post, from where it continued its predation of our mouse field.

The next day it was still there and Larry had an inspiration. He caught a mouse and went out near the barn and held the mouse up by the tail and started calling "hawk, hawk, hawk". It didn't take hawk more than ten seconds to spot the mouse and down it came, straight for Larry. At the last second he broke, dropped the mouse and ducked. Hawk turned on its back as it went past, snatched the mouse out of the air, completed its barrel role and flew up to the barn roof with its meal.

Well that started something. Dad's only problem was keeping us working. Every chance we got we fed the hawk. We went to using gloves and trying to hold on to the mouse without flinching while hawk plucked it out of our fingers. It never touched us and soon we were using bare hands. Even when hawk was not in sight, we could get a mouse or a sparrow, stand in the field and holler "hawk, hawk, hawk" and within a minute you would suddenly see this huge bird hurtling at you shoulder high at an unnerving speed. Sometimes it came from behind and you heard nothing until the slight pluck at your fingers told you that hawk had struck again.

I had a girl friend from the city, and on her next visit we shot a sparrow, which didn't please her at all. Next thing was to persuade her to hold it up shoulder high by the tail out at arms length. This was a very difficult thing to accomplish without telling her why. Then Larry said he would call a hawk out of the air to take the sparrow.

Now she knew we were playing some stupid trick on her but had no idea what, so she put on a long suffering expression and stood there feeling stupid while Larry called "hawk, hawk, hawk". About thirty seconds went by and she had just about had enough when she suddenly spotted hawk about twenty metres away coming at her at about 60 kph. Her eyes bugged out, then slammed shut and she let out a scream that I would not have believed possible. It didn't bother hawk. He turned a half barrel roll, plucked the sparrow delicately from her fingers, rolled back up and flew to the barn to dine.

June was still standing frozen to the spot, the tail feathers of the sparrow still clutched in her fingers. In retrospect it was a stupid trick, but we had no idea what kind of a shock we were subjecting her to. She didn't have a heart attack or anything like that but she never trusted me again.

When fall came, hawk joined the rest of his clan in the migration south. He never returned the next spring. Dad pointed out that he probably tried to adopt some American farmer down south who would immediately have shot him as an overly aggressive chicken hawk. It was fun while it lasted but things like that never have happy endings.

TOBY

I don't own a dog. I did once and that's why I never would again. I got Toby when I was about twelve, living on the Eastern outskirts of Saskatoon. There weren't any rules then about dogs so Toby became an appendage. Playing or hunting or running around the prairie on foot or on bikes, Toby went where I went. He was a little black mongrel that my Dad picked up somewhere. About twenty pounds of stupidity.

Smart enough in some ways. Like the time I was cycling past a local farm and a chicken went squawking across the road in front of us. Toby had that bird in a flash and started shaking the life out of it. I was horrified. If the farmer saw, he'd just grab a gun and shoot Toby on the spot, and then charge me for the chicken.

I jumped off my bike and started beating Toby unmercifully until he dropped the bird, which went flapping off screaming and yelling, apparently none the worse for its mauling. I whopped Toby a few more times and then jumped on my bike and got out of there. Toby followed along with a kind of quizzical expression on his face, obviously wondering about the incomprehensible behaviour of small boys. Of course he wasn't hurt. An open hand on a fur coat doesn't do much damage other than psychological.

But for the rest of his life he took a wide detour around any chicken he ever saw. Forget ever making a retriever out of him. One lesson was enough.

Toby had defective vision. He could not distinguish size. Any dog that came within sight (other than his friends of course) was attacked. Whether it was a Pekinese or a German Shepherd made no difference. He attacked a Saint Bernard once. The big dog, about the size of a Shetland pony, put a paw on top of him, squashing him flat and looked soulfully at me as if to say "would you please remove this little rat?"

A German Shepherd is a different problem. We met one of those one day with the usual result. Toby upside down staring at a set of pearly white, bone crushing teeth. Given the snarl that went with the teeth, and the fact that the dog was bigger than me, really gave me second thoughts about rescuing my friend. Fortunately the big dog was not hungry and after a few meaningful snarls let Toby up. Unfortunately, Toby took this as a sign of weakness and attacked again. This little charade went on three times before I got up enough nerve to get close enough to get a hand on Toby, whereupon the Shepherd gave me an indignant look, shook his head and went on his way.

Toby got distemper one day and my Dad said that there was nothing to do but put him out of his misery. Now you might as well have told me my brother or sister were sick so we would have to kill them and bury them in the back yard. I dug in my heels. Rather than be the cause of such trauma himself, Dad said what I should do is take Toby to the vet at the University, to see if she could fix him up. Of course he was sure she would put the dog to sleep and that would be the end of it.

It turned out she had a soft spot for small boys and dogs. I still remember her face, which was the kindest thing I ever saw. I remember her forearms. More muscle than my Dad and he had been a lumberjack. She took Toby in her big hands and he never budged, a miracle in itself. She looked him over and prodded him here and there and then said: "you know he is likely going to die, but I have a new drug we are just testing, sulphathiazole (or something like that). We'll just try it and you can bring him back in a week to see what we should do." She took a tiny tube of yellow stuff and rubbed it in his eyes and then made him swallow a pill. To do that you had to open his jaws (that's where the forearm muscles came in) and shove the pill down his throat till he gagged and had to swallow it. That meant putting your hand in between all those teeth. I was supposed to do that for five days, and rub the ointment in his eyes too.

Well, the dog put up with that and I didn't lose any fingers. He recovered, and my Dad went to the vet and asked how much we had to pay. She said it was just research and the University could afford that. There are some saints in the world.

Toby was still with us when I got my first car. It was an old 1930 Buick and fortunately the tires were soft. I had only driven our even older 1926 Chevy and of course I was pretty excited. Dad parked it in front of the house and I got into the drivers seat and started it up. Now Toby was left out and was beside himself, but I didn't notice. I put it in gear and drove off. I felt the tires on the drivers side go bump, bump over something and then I saw Toby in the rear view running for home, yipping all the way.

When we found him he was under my bed and I never forgot the look on his face. He thought I had punished him terribly for something and he didn't even know what. I was sixteen then and should have listened to my Dad who said he was in pain and we really had to put him away. I couldn't face that, so Dad said OK, but he'll be dead in the morning anyway and you'll feel even worse.

Well, he wasn't dead in the morning. The wheels must have passed over his mid section without actually rupturing anything. I fed him milk and bread under my bed for three days and cleaned up after him before he finally crawled out. We couldn't touch him anywhere for another week but then he came around and was soon running as though nothing had happened. My Dad just shook his head and said; "that's not a dog, that's a cat and even he must be running out of lives."

Five years later we moved to the farm, and Toby wasn't a farm dog. He never learned about porcupines. The first day he came home with his mouth and tongue full of bristles my Dad said once more that he had had it. The quills would eventually work their way into some vital organ and he would be dead. Better to just put a bullet in him now.

My brother (six years younger but a lot bigger than me) agreed to help so the two of us cornered Toby and Larry held him while I got the pliers and pulled out about thirty quills. It must have been like getting teeth pulled without any freezing. A couple of days later he was eating again as though nothing had happened.

That wasn't the end of it though. About every third week he would go looking for a porcupine to exact his revenge, with predictable results. Thank God he didn't pick skunks as an adversary. He would then come whining to me and sit there while I pulled out all the quills. He may have been stupid but he had guts.

The tale does not have a happy ending. The farm went bankrupt. My family moved to Edmonton and I found a job with the Post Office in Saskatoon. I could only afford a boarding house and they would not allow dogs. Farm neighbours took Toby but he was too old to change owners. One night about thirty below I was driving out to Taylor's farm when I met this apparition on the road. A little dog, completely covered in frost, trotting along the shoulder toward Saskatoon still fifteen miles away. Of course it was Toby. He must have decided that we had all gone back to our old home in Saskatoon and he was headed in there to find us.

I took him into the car and his joy was heartbreaking. I had betrayed him. My whole family had betrayed him. Did he hold that against us? Of course not. Dogs don't have that sort of mentality. No matter what you do to them they still love you.

I was of course powerless. If you don't have money in our world you are tied to your fate. I took him back to Taylor's place, had supper with them and then had to leave. Toby couldn't believe I was not going to take him with me. Mrs. Taylor held him and said he would be alright once I was gone. I still remember the look on his face when I went out the door.

A week later Mrs. Taylor phoned and said she had let Toby out to relieve himself and he hadn't come back in. She assumed he had taken off for Saskatoon again. My brother and I got in the car and headed out there but we didn't meet him this time. We never saw him again.

No. I don't own a dog. The responsibility is too great.

VIENNA

The Parents Day Hike

I spent two years as a Scouter with American Troop 427 in Vienna, Austria, where I had the curious experience of being labelled an alien, forbidden to take part in the opening and closing ceremonies, which involved allegiance to the American flag. So much for the World Brotherhood of Scouting. It wasn't really so bad as all that. The Americans are used to referring to all other nationalities as aliens and it doesn't bring pictures of green, two headed beings with tentacles for arms to their minds. In any case, that's not what this story is about.

One tradition of the troop was an annual trek to the place where we had overnight camps. Everyone took part in this ritual; cubs, scouts, parents and little brothers and sisters, so it was quite a caravan wending its way through the Wienerwald, the Vienna Woods in English.

It was not an insignificant physical challenge. The Wienerwald is the Eastern tip of the Alps and consists of a series of high, forested ridges that curl around Vienna like the tail of a sea horse. This topography causes Alpine winds to form a vortex over the city, bringing some of the most miserable foggy, cold, wet, windy weather imaginable.

The hike always started from the American International School, which borders the Wienerwald. Walking these heavily forested ridges is an Austrian tradition in which the whole population takes part, so there are well established paths wandering everywhere. The particular path to the scout campsite led off through a vast deciduous forest, up over one ridge, down into a valley with a paved road at the bottom, and up to the crest of another ridge where we held our camps. The campsite was an open field completely exposed to the wind and rain. We were not allowed to camp in the forest for fear of starting forest fires, so campfires were always a real challenge.

The plan for the day was simple. The hike itself was about six kilometres, which, over that terrain with a lot of little kids took up the whole day, so we didn't need any program. The older scouts led off. They were supposed to get to the site first, light a fire and have hot dogs and tea ready for the rest of the caravan as they arrived. Younger scouts, including my two sons, followed with the first aid kit which always accompanied outings like this. Being American it was an excellent kit, probably capable of supporting major surgery in the hands of a competent field surgeon. I and my wife Margaret followed the scouts, then came the rest of the caravan with the other scouters bringing up the rear to make sure no one got lost.

It was always a problem to decide exactly where the first aid kit should be with a caravan that stretched a couple of kilometres. Since the scouts were moving fastest it was decided that they were most likely to have accidents, particularly burnt fingers making the tea and hot dogs, so the kit went with them.

When Margaret and I arrived it was evident we were in some trouble. A howling wind was blowing a fine mist across our clearing at about 40 kilometres an hour. The scouts were wet and had been unable to light the fire and people were arriving. Embarrassing! Particularly for two Chief Scouts who theoretically were prepared by their training for anything.

Old Scouter to the rescue. Set a couple of scouts splitting wood thin to get to the dry part. Use the first aid box as a wind break, assisted by four scouts huddled on either side, trying to form a wall. Lots of small kindling and presto, the fire took. With the amount of fresh air blowing past, the fire roared, the tea was soon made and everyone, with only minor delay, was eating their hot dog and drinking strong sweet tea to fuel up for the trip back to the school.

That's where the day started to go wrong. With that wet hurricane blowing across our mountain ridge, people were not about to wait for the whole caravan to assemble before starting back. By the time everyone was fed, I finally tumbled to the fact that half of them were already gone, including a lot of scouts. Not wanting the caravan to lose it's integrity completely, I sent the rest of the scouts on ahead with the first aid kit, with instructions to get to the head of the line and try to slow people down so we wouldn't be too spread out if someone got into difficulty. Margaret and I would bring up the rear and collect stragglers. It sounded sensible to me at the time.

After putting the campfire out and checking the area for litter, Margaret and I started back alone. About a kilometre down we caught up with an older Argentinean diplomat dressed in suit and tie and overcoat, his much younger wife in a full length fur coat and their twin 11 year old cubs. I was not the only alien in this international troop. I mention the dress because in Europe people don't hike the mountain trails in their old clothes. They dress up in their Sunday best.

The trail towards the bottom of the first valley was quite steep and rain had washed part of it into a muddy gully about two metres deep leaving only a narrow footpath between the gully and the trees.

The light was starting to fade and I was getting worried because the tail end of this procession consisted of the youngest kids and their parents who were not all familiar with the branching network of trails. I had no way of knowing where the scouts were and whether or not they had succeeded in organizing the rest of the parade into any kind of order. The diplomat finally suggested that I go ahead to make sure no one got lost. He knew the trail and would have no difficulty getting his family back on his own before dark.

Agreeing that we would wait at the school to make sure they got back safely, Margaret and I started to hurry to catch up to two more cubs far ahead who seemed to be on their own. We hadn't gone more than fifty metres when a scream from behind stopped us cold. Then the Argentinean's voice rose in a wail. "I've broken my leg!"

Not pleasant. I looked down the trail and the two cubs had disappeared. Shit! We scrambled back up the trail to find the diplomat lying in the muddy trench. His legs were together and straight and I prayed for only a sprained ankle. When I got down to him the first thing I saw was bone splinters sticking out through his right pant leg. Shit again.

He was a big man and with nothing to immobilize the leg there was no hope of getting him out of the mud in that trench. He was wedged in so you couldn't even get anything under him. The first aid kit with all that fancy equipment? Long gone. How long would they wait at the school before coming back three or four kilometres to find us? In the dark? Too long. We had really screwed up. The first aid kit should have brought up the rear, with the biggest guys for stretcher bearers.

We had some luck but not much. I knew there was a house on the road that ran through the valley at the bottom of this trail, about a kilometre farther down. Margaret agreed to take the lady and two kids down to the house and phone and ambulance. Neither of the women could speak German but those two little kids could speak Spanish, English and German.

Away they went but it wasn't easy going. The mother went into shock after they left and kept fainting, so it took them a while to get to the house. The kids explained the situation and an ambulance was called. In the meantime I sat in the mud and talked to the victim. He stayed conscious the whole time, even when I took off his belt and tied his two feet together to stop the spasms in his leg from doing more damage. Thankfully no major blood vessel was cut so there wasn't much bleeding.

It got dark and time dragged on. I couldn't believe that no one had come back to look for us. Finally we heard voices. German voices. And then a light and behind it Margaret, the two cubs and two stretcher bearers. The ambulance had obviously come from the city. The men were in uniform with street shoes and of course spoke no English, so the kids translated. Getting that heavy man on to the stretcher in the bottom of that trench was not easy and it must have been torture for him but he took it in silence, I guess to save his kids any more stress than they were already under. Fortunately the stretcher had a blanket because he was by now shuddering violently from shock and hypothermia.

I had hiking boots on so I took one end of the stretcher. We couldn't get up out of that trench, particularly with the two attendants in street shoes, so had to slip and slither down that hill till it ended. It was a nightmare but the diplomat kept talking to his kids all the way down. Not until we slid the stretcher into the ambulance did he let go and pass out. His wife went with him and we kept the twins, promising to take them home where their housekeeper would take them in.

The people from the house at the bottom of the valley invited us in while they called a taxi. I wondered how often they had played that role for injured hikers. We went in to their living room and had just sat down in our mud splattered clothes when the biggest dog I had ever seen rose up from behind the couch. It looked like a German Shepherd the size of a shetland pony. The lady of the house said something and it lay down again. We had no common language but when she said "schnapps?" we knew that much german and said in unison, "ja! schnapps bitte". That's Austrian white lightning and we needed it.

The taxi came and we took the twins home and then went home ourselves. We didn't bother going to the school because obviously we had been deserted by everyone including our own two sons. At the door our oldest, Peter, said "where did you guys go?" I said "it's a long story. Where's Gordon?"

"Gordon? Everyone went home but that twit wouldn't come. He went back up the trail to look for you".

Gordon was twelve and was back somewhere in the woods in the dark without even a flashlight. I grabbed a flashlight and was just heading out the door myself when the phone rang. It was Gordon. An accusing tone on the edge of tears - "where did you go? You never came back to the school."

"Never mind that now, Gordon. Where are you?"

"I don't know, but there's this big dog here."

"Gordon, I know where you are. Just stay there. I'll be out to get you in twenty minutes."

I suppose all's well that ends well but you can believe the lecture that the scouts and the other leaders got at the next meeting, about staying together and how useful a first aid kit is back in the school, and how nobody ever goes home till everyone is accounted for. I used that story in every troop I was with from then on to illustrate that rules are not just so many words to be forgotten when it's late and cold and everyone is miserable and just want to go home to a warm meal and bed.

Ottawa Adventures

Charge Certificate

No, a Charge Certificate is not a reward for running up a big bill on your VISA card. It's a curious name for a card that says you have passed the requirements that authorize you to take scout troops on canoe trips. If my experience is any indication, a guy with a charge certificate has been put through the mill and you can trust your kid to his tender mercies for anything up to a week in a canoe.

The first thing you need is a St. John's emergency first aid certificate. After that you take a water rescue course. In my case that involved things like practising mouth to mouth resuscitation in the water while trying to get the body into a canoe. Not a dummy either. A real live body who is playing dead. No sanitary mouth pieces for us. The guy I got (this was an all male cast; stop dreaming about getting paired with a girl guide leader) was about 100 kg with a big moustache. I couldn't lift one arm into the canoe let alone the whole body so I had to hang over the side giving mouth to mouth upside down while my partner tried to paddle this anchor to shore. My victim didn't breathe on his own either, which takes some kind of control when my lungs were only half the size of his. And that moustache! Ugh! In real life I'd have let him drown.

Maybe they don't do things like that any more, what with AIDS and all, but it is an eye opener. Thirty seconds into the game and you forget it's just make believe. Panic sets in when you realize you may not be up to the task. It is not a pleasant experience but you don't forget it either.

The end of this course was a three day canoe trip to test out everything you had learned. Ours took place out of Ontario's provincial scout camp, Opemekon, on Christie Lake near Perth. The Tay river runs out of Bob's Lake into Christie and you can make a circuit by crossing Christie to the

Tay, paddling up into Bob's, portaging over into a series of puddles and finally portaging back into Christie. It was designed by a sadist.

There is a dam at the outlet from Bob's lake and there is no way around it. Approaching from the downstream end you run out of water a kilometre below the dam. No, you don't line the canoes from shore; there is no shore. The dam is always closed now because they don't run logs down the Tay any more and it keeps the water level in Bob's lake high for all the cottagers there, who don't like their docks to be left high and dry. Therefor the stream below the dam is silted in with waist deep stinking mud.

When you are finished with the Humphrey Bogart bit you are faced with seven metres of concrete with sheer rock on both sides. Nothing for it but to scale this obstacle and haul the packs and canoes over with ropes. In the spring the water is near the top of the dam and you can easily (in a relative sense) launch the canoes from the concrete. In the fall after a dry summer the water can be two metres below the top and you have to rope the canoes down and then climb down ropes to get into them.

Fortunately, our trip was in the spring, so the dam was only a one way obstacle. I took some scouts on the circuit in reverse in the fall after a dry summer, but that's another story. Thank God for two big, strong sons, stupid enough to go with me on these jaunts. I suspect they thought Dad wouldn't survive on his own and they needed his income for university.

The Tay wasn't enough of a challenge for our charge certificate group. The night we arrived at Opemekon about 7 o'clock the sky was turning black and ugly. The clouds were rolling in a way that had everyone standing staring at them and thinking maybe we'll just wait in the cars for awhile. The air was dead calm with a kind of greenish light that made the rolling clouds even more menacing. And then the buses arrived.

Five school buses full of cubs. They disgorged in all directions and the buses turned and fled. Then somebody yelled that there was a tornado warning and everyone should take cover. Sure. Where? And then it hit.

It wasn't pitch dark but dark enough to obscure the surroundings and then the rain fell and the wind screamed and trees started coming down. Panicked cub leaders were trying desperately to round up their charges and find somewhere to take them. There were cabins down the hill through the trees but the trees were not exactly a safe haven. We scouters ran around assisting as best we could and when they were all headed toward the cabins and what we hoped was safety we headed back to the cars to wait it out.

It was nearly dark now and the wind still screamed and the rain bucketed down. Half way across the clearing to my car this little form appeared out of the muck. "Are you an akela?" it said. I squatted down to see better what I had and said "no, son. What pack are you with?" He gave me the number and even which cabin they were assigned. He wasn't even worried, just temporarily misplaced and I stood there in that wild night and marvelled at such self assurance in such a little body. I offered to take him to the cabin and he thanked me politely and off we went as though the world was not trying to come to an end.

A distraught Akela was just leaving the cabin, having discovered that one of his flock was missing in that awful blackness out there. You want to see a man just pardoned from the gallows at the last second? He avoided breaking down in tears but only just.

There was a tornado that night that wiped out a nearby town, but we didn't get the full punch. I don't want to get any closer to one though. Our original plan had been to leave that night and camp on an island in Christie Lake. When we got there the next morning there was an eighty foot poplar blown down across the small space that was cleared for tents. We would all have been under that if we had arrived at Opemekon an hour earlier, and one cub would have spent a bad night in the bush, his Akela a worse night in the cabin, or lost himself in the bush.

The Tay River Run

Charge certificate in hand, I proceeded to teach scouts canoe tripping. Actually I had been doing that for a long time but these were new rules, prompted by the canoeing disaster on lake Temiskaming in which many young boys died of exposure. Not Boy Scouts, but they could have been. Their leaders were experienced but they were supposed to be challenging these kids. Staying alive is more important and avoiding challenge that is also dangerous is the new rule.

My first trip duly authorized by my charge certificate came unexpectedly in late October of the same year. I had an enthusiastic group of boys who had spent many summer evenings passing all the requirements for their gold stage canoeing proficiency badge. They had one canoe trip to do that had to be 30 k and include two nights camping.

I pointed out that winter was at hand, the leaves had all fallen and it had already snowed once. The canoe trip would have to wait till the spring. They pointed out in turn that they would be old men by spring, maybe dead, or maybe moved away. They also pointed out that they had been to camp Opemekon and knew that the camp had lots of canoes and would lend them to us.

I caved in and said "OK, OK, but you guys have to make all the arrangements, contact the camp, get the food, everything! I'll go along if you get all that done and the weather looks good."

Of course they did. I got a call from Headquarters asking if I really wanted to do this. I said if the boys had made all the arrangements I didn't have much choice. The camp was closed for the season but some Venturers were still up there closing up and would get five canoes out for us. If we did the circuit in reverse we could even use the camp transporter to cover the first portage to the chain of little lakes that would take us to Bob's Lake. We wouldn't have to face that one at the end if the weather turned bad.

I asked my two sons, who were Venturers at the time, full grown and a lot bigger than me, if they would like to come along. They got the message all right. Dad was afraid to handle it without them. I'm not proud. A lot of muscle is good insurance even if it is a bit condescending.

Friday I checked the weather and it was unbelievably good for late October so off we went. The first night we got the canoes over the portage to the first little lake and camped there. Saturday morning dawned bright and clear and all the worries about winter disappeared in the beautiful fall sunshine. The water was pretty low and we had a bad time getting ashore at the last portage before the big one into Bob's Lake. The time was getting on so we decided to make camp and face the portage in the morning.

The campsite was flat and grassy, with lots of firewood for cooking and a campfire. Just what scouting is all about, and we turned in knowing that God was in his heaven and all was right with the world.

We woke up to 10 cm of snow, overcast, a North wind and unbelievably, dense fog. Breakfast wasn't quite so cheerful but I said, "hey guys, a bonus. You get to claim this as a winter camp for your winter camping badge." That helped a bit. But then we got to the portage.

Finding it in that fog presented another unexpected challenge. The portage started beside a general store which made it easy, but we couldn't find the store. After several futile passes along the shoreline, I finally got out, traversed north till I hit the road and then walked along it to find the store. The store wasn't there. It had burned down two nights before.

One thing I had forgotten is that there is a hundred foot ridge between Bob's Lake and the chain we were on, most of it on our side. We soon found another problem. The Venturers back at camp had given us old Peterborough wood and canvas canoes. The canvas had long since rotted and been replaced with fibre glass. They weighed about 45 kg and our scouts weighed about half that. We had to transport them one at a time. After the first one, slipping and sliding in the wet snow, it was evident that the boys would be lucky if they could get their packs over so I and my sons heaved the last four over the ridge. It was lunch time by the time we embarked on Bob's Lake but I said we had to make the dam before lunch or we would run out of daylight before we got back to Opemekon. Prophets are made, not born.

When we got to the dam the water was two metres below the top on the upstream side and seven metres on the downstream side. The top of the dam was only about a metre thick with no possibility of detouring around it. This was a learning experience not to be missed. I asked if they knew what being committed meant, which of course they didn't. I then said that we were now committed to go over the dam. When the arguments started I asked what other option was there. You got it. Back over that portage in the snow and slush, through a couple of swamps and arrive at the last long portage in the dark with no transporter to get those monstrous canoes back to the camp.

Right. We were committed to go over the dam. Once over it was just a matter of paddling downstream a few kilometres, across Christie Lake and back to the Van. They didn't know about the kilometre of mud below the dam and I didn't tell them.

We had ropes with us because I knew about the dam. But it took all of us grunting and heaving to get those old canoes up that two metre wall and down the seven metre wall on the other side. Four of them had to stay at the bottom to catch the canoes and two had to stay in the canoes above the dam to tie on the next one. That left me, my sons and the biggest scout to haul eight overweight canoes up one side and down the other. No lunch yet and it was two o'clock.

Well, there was nowhere to stop at the bottom so we piled in and paddled off; for about one hundred metres until we ran out of water. The boys tried poling through the muck but soon realized that there was only one way. Get out and pull. It was not warm mud and by the time we were out on dry ground no one felt like lunch.

Lesson number two. No matter how tired and cold and wet you are, you have to eat or you won't make it. So we got fires going and made a hot lunch. Everyone drank strong sweet coffee, some for the first time in their lives.

By the time we were all in the canoes once more spirits were again high. No more obstacles. Just paddle over to Opemekon and get in the Van and Scouter would drive everybody home. Unfortunately it was four o'clock and starting to get dark. That fact dawned on them by the time we reached the lake and they had no idea where Opemekon was. Of course I knew but I wasn't about to tell them. Scouts never take compass work seriously. It's too much like school work. You have to get them cornered before it gets through that if they can't plot a course they're not going to get home. I was exhausted and so was everybody else but I and my sons just sat there and said that they had the map and compass and could read it as well as we could.

A couple of them finally got the map out and found where we were with the aid of a flashlight, and then where Opemekon was. It took a while to figure out what the compass bearing was and then to figure out how to set the compass to point at Opemekon. When they did all you could see was a dark shore against a somewhat lighter sky. No lights any where. They were not very confident about heading out into the lake for a point that only the compass told them was Opemekon.

I suggested we could make camp here on the shore and wait for morning, with no supper and no breakfast and everything soaking wet. No response to that. They just started paddling.

It was a bit touchy when we raised the far shore because the beach wasn't there. Which way had we missed and by how far? All you could see now was the vague skyline of the shore on the opposite side of the bay. One boy said we had to paddle to the right which started the arguments going. I finally asked if anyone knew for sure which way we had to go. Only the first kid said yes, so I suggested we go for it.

The beach came into focus about half a kilometre farther on. I asked our guide how he was so sure. It turned out he had been at camp that summer and had noticed a sheer rock face across the bay and just to the right. There was some graffiti on it that had caught his eye. When we hit shore you could see the outline of that peak straight across the water and he knew if we were at the beach it would have been off to the right. Good observation and good memory and the courage of his conviction. Good patrol leader qualities. Now if only he could learn to tie knots.

A canoe trip is not over till the gear is all stowed and you had to be there to hear the moans and groans. The canoes had to be carried about two hundred metres and put on their racks in the shed. The packs had to be stacked in the van carefully in order to get everything in and all the boys seated with seat belts fastened.

Then the van wouldn't start. Well, it was old and tired and often needed persuasion which this time took me about fifteen minutes. The cheers when it finally caught were heartfelt.

Did that experience turn them off of canoe tripping? Not likely. The moaning they were able to do to their parents about how they had suffered. The bragging they were able to do at troop meeting about how tough they were and what incredible obstacles they had overcome. The prestige they enjoyed with the younger scouts who now looked up to them in awe.

On the other hand, no one ever suggested doing the Tay Run again.

The Big Log Campfire

There is no such thing as a boring winter camp. Camps that don't include cabins at any rate. Outside with only your sleeping bag, clothes and ingenuity for protection you are so busy surviving that there is little time for anything else. You might not notice from the safety of your warm house, but good weather that lasts more than 24 hours in winter is a rare phenomenon. Snow, rain, wind, sleet, whiteout; you name it, it happens.

Ontario is particularly bad because it is always wet if it is not twenty or thirty below and there is rarely enough snow to build effective shelters. You survive on the strength of your knowledge and what you can carry on your back or toboggan.

I always cheated a bit. The boys have to believe they are on their own or they take the easy way out. On the other hand, safety considerations dictate that you need an escape hatch. Occasionally you meet a kid who insists on toughing it out even if a warm cabin is right beside him. These kids don't necessarily make good leaders. They are interested in proving something to themselves, not in exerting power over anyone else. They are always tough but often loners.

My cheating was to take them on a route that seemed to go off into the wilderness but ended up within half a kilometre of my cottage.

This particular camp Peter Scarlett and I and a dozen kids left the truck on the East side of White lake, packed our toboggans and trekked two kilometres across the lake and then another up a small creek into a beaver swamp where there were a lot of dead trees sticking up out of the ice.

Scouts always complain that we won't let them make big campfires so this time I was going to cure that. Many places where scouts camp will no longer allow fires at all and boys only learn to use camp stoves, which doesn't really satisfy the primeval urge to build wood fires.

Learned men like to speculate about the discovery of fire. They even made a movie about it. I think homo sapiens always built fires just like the birds build nests. It is an inborn instinct and no one ever discovered it for the first time.

We never used tents on winter camps. Tents are for keeping rain and bugs off. We did carry tarps in case we couldn't find natural windbreaks. They also come in handy when it rains, as it often does in Ontario in the winter. We also didn't camp as patrols. Each boy was self contained and had his own bed, his own cooking fire and his own food. If you camp in patrols, one or two advanced scouts end up doing everything and the others sit around and watch, which I don't think is the most effective approach.

To my mind self sufficiency is most important. Many others feel that encouraging leadership is the essential thing. The trouble is that to have leaders you need a lot of followers and I wasn't interested in training followers. The leaders will discover themselves once they gain proficiency.

By mid afternoon everyone was established in his own little winter camp; bedroll, kitchen, latrine and wind break, either natural or tarp lashed securely to trees. So I called them in to discuss the next move.

"Do you want a campfire?"

„Yay! Yah! A big campfire!"

"You know what the Indians said. 'White man build big fire, stand far away and freeze. Indian build small fire, huddle close and stay warm.'"

"We're not cold. We want a big camp fire. Big!"

"OK, get the cross cut saw and come with me. Everyone!"

We went out onto the pond where the dead trees stood and I selected one about twenty metres high and thirty cm in diameter and set them to it. Fifteen minutes later they were back complaining that the tree was too big. "No, no", I said. "It's just right. We want big logs."

It took them the rest of the afternoon and evening to cut that tree into metre lengths and notch the logs so they could be stacked into a log cabin type fire. They then collected the branches, broke them up and filled the centre of the structure. Finally a platform was laid on top with a nice little teepee of kindling and birch bark tinder.

After supper, when everyone had their camp ready so they just had to undress and crawl in (you don't want to do that chore in the dark) we gathered around this colossus of logs and with fitting ceremony the youngest scout got to strike the match and light the birch bark.

A log cabin style fire starts very slowly and lasts a long time because it has to burn down from the top rather than up from the bottom. It gets bigger as it burns and ends with a roaring fire. We played charades and sang a bit. This was the only group I ever had that liked charades and they were good. They would play at this for a couple of hours on a good night. Kids that can entertain themselves are a scouter's dream.

Soon the coals from the top were filtering down into the pile. They hadn't been careful to build solid layers of cross logs which are supposed to keep the fire at each level until it is nearly burned off before the one below it catches. Soon two levels were burning at once and the snow around was starting to melt. Then three levels, and then the bottom level caught so that all five levels got going. There was no danger because with a foot of snow over everything no one was going to start a forest fire, and the thing was built on the ice of the pond to boot.

The Indians were right. Soon everyone was backing up, fronts roasting in the heat and backs freezing. I started to hear rumblings about BIG LOGS, and whose idea was this anyway? As Robert Service said in The Cremation of Sam Magee, "the fire soared and the furnace roared, such a sight you seldom see".

When everyone was tired and wanted to crawl into their sleeping bags the fire still roared. I pointed out that it couldn't spread from where it was so we could just let it burn out, and so the BIG LOG campfire ended. When I got up to relieve myself at one AM there was still a heap of glowing coals floating on a raft of logs in a steadily deepening pit in the ice. By morning it had drowned itself.

Not that there was anything to see in the morning. As I said, winter camping is always full of surprises. The place where we were camped was on a stream that emptied into the lake half a kilometre East. A storm had moved in from the East and the wind funnelled up the stream and onto us. In retrospect not the best choice for a campsite. Snow in the form of ice pellets was coming down so hard you could not look into the wind.

The pellets were like little ball bearings and rolled into everything. Poke your head out of the sleeping bag and a handful of pellets would roll down to your bum, the lowest part of the bag. Needless to say we were not long in getting up. It was a bad scene. No one escaped a pant full of melting ice balls and although the temperature had come up to near freezing, the combination of wind and wet soon had everyone shivering in their boots. There was no way we could find the fireplaces, let alone light a fire to cook breakfast. An attempt to raise a windbreak in that gale was soon abandoned.

Time to bail out. We packed the toboggans as best we could and I led off. I got some argument because I was heading deeper into the bush and the boys were all for getting back to the parking lot. There was no possibility of that because it was three kilometres straight into that blinding wind across a trackless lake. Even if we found it there was only my van there and not enough room to get everyone in. Furthermore, the snow ploughs would not even come till the snow stopped coming down. "Trust me", I said.

My cottage was only 500 metres away but it was a bedraggled lot that dragged themselves in. One kid was worried that we shouldn't go into someone's cottage without permission and we discussed that for a bit, noting that if life was at risk, no one would refuse us shelter. Then one of them asked how we were going to get in. He didn't want to break any windows.

I then said "just watch," and pulled out my key and unlocked the door. Of course it then dawned on them that it was my cottage and I had tricked them into thinking they were far from civilization.

We soon had a fire going and clothes drying while we cooked breakfast. By this time they were all claiming that they could have made it even without help and each one had a plan for what he would have done. No harm in that but the truth is that some things can not be overcome by small boys in winter. If you are responsible you better have a safe line of retreat.

The snow stopped about noon and we packed up and assembled at the beach. There was not a track of any kind on the lake and of course none of them had thought to fix a landmark on the other shore when we had left the day before. They all looked at me, but I said it was their problem.

They were supposed to know how to find their way back. They all had compasses.

With much reluctance they found their compasses and after looking blankly at the far shore and back at the compasses it soon became clear that the instrument was of no use whatsoever if you didn't know where you were and where you wanted to go. Finally one of them came and said they couldn't do anything because they didn't have a map.

"Ah ha!" I said. "I have a map. How come no one else brought one?"

"No fair, scouter. We didn't know we were going to get lost."

So I gave them the map. It took a while before they came to the conclusion they were still lost because with a map and a compass they still didn't know where on the map they were. They weren't enthused about more lectures but you need a situation like this to get the point across that there is a reason to learn map reading and compass, and that you have to know where you went if you want to find your way back. You can not just teach that out of a book. I was in no hurry because I knew the cars couldn't get in to pick us up, and of course all the parents knew we were near my cottage so they wouldn't be worried either.

I finally showed them where my cottage was on the map and where the parking lot was. But no one had brought a scouting manual and they couldn't remember which way declination went. East or West. In our part of Ontario, declination is 10 degrees, so if you get it wrong you are 20 degrees out which in a few kilometres can get you very lost.

They took sights on the far shore with both readings of declination and quickly learned that if they chose the wrong one they could be a long way from the parking lot and with all this new snow they didn't need an extra kilometre of hard slogging.

Another learning experience. The information you need is all on every topographical map. Of course there aren't step by step instructions but once I had pointed out the compass rose at the bottom of the map they finally got it right and found the parking lot just before the snowplough arrived with all the cars.

The story the parents got was of course how the storm had got them lost but they had found their way back with map and compass. No problem.

The Beaver Pond

We had another winter camp on the same beaver pond but this was with a group of older scouts, one of whom was a polio survivor. He couldn't carry a back pack because one shoulder was deformed and he couldn't pull a toboggan because one leg was deformed. But he was tough and he wanted to get his winter camping badge. He carried a sort of satchel that he could hang on his good shoulder and he dragged himself along in the trail left by the toboggans. The other guys were used to him and didn't offer to help unless asked, and he rarely asked.

The day we went across the lake was cold and clear. Just the kind of winter day that God makes to show you it is great to be alive. We had no particular problem getting to the beaver pond and cut down a dead tree for firewood, made lunch and prepared camp for the night. The sun was even warm if you found a sheltered spot to sit and soak it up.

There were five kids and my son and I. Four of them decided they would bed down together in a bit of a hollow, using each other for warmth. The polio boy had no mattress since he had to travel as light as possible so we all pitched in to collect pine and spruce bows for his bed. That sounds easy but it takes a lot of small bows to make a bed that you can actually get any sleep on. I don't recommend the practice for scouts because a dozen boys would have to strip an acre of trees to get bedded down.

My son and I spread our toboggans out a bit apart. The guys like to talk at night and the conversation is not for scouters ears. They don't know that scouters were once scouts and have already heard it all.

We didn't stay up long. When the sun set the temperature dropped like a bomb. It was one of those nights that is dead calm and so clear that the stars fill the sky till they are almost hard to look at. The milky way stood out like a band of cloud and the words of Robert Service echoed in my head; "and the stars came out and they danced about". It's not often that you can see the colours of stars but this night they sparkled like diamonds and reflected all the colours of the rainbow.

And the temperature dropped. About midnight I woke with a chill in my middle and got up to pee. In just my underwear the cold, as Service said, "stabbed like a driven nail." I checked all the guys and they were all sleeping, or at least they were quiet. I checked my son and he was awake.

"How's it going?" I asked.

"It's bloody cold, that's what it is."

This was a long speech for my son, and if he was cold then everyone was going to be cold. Seven more hours till daylight. If it got too bad I could always light the fire I had laid before going to bed. This was a small fire within reach of my sleeping bag. It had a big pot of tea already brewed and sweetened hung over it. Come morning I could reach out one hand, light the tinder, and snuggle back down until the tea was ready to drink.

Everyone would be able to get up then, get dressed, have a cup of hot tea and then keep alive till morning cutting more wood. It's not a good solution. If you need a fire for warmth you are in trouble. That only works for one night. If you had a second night to put in exhaustion would catch up to you and it would be game over. Stay dry, stay fed and get your rest is the only way to stay alive in the winter unless you have artificial shelter.

I crawled back in to my bag with some misgivings. The last time I had seen a night like this was back in Saskatoon many years before when my assistant had lost his toes to frostbite.

About one in the morning I was startled awake with what seemed like an earthquake. I was sure the ground had moved. I lay and listened but no other sound. The stars still glittered overhead. Then "whump!" And the earth shuddered again. It took a minute and then it dawned. The ice on the pond was expanding in the cold and when it built up enough pressure it would shift a bit on the rocks. How cold did it have to get to cause that? I didn't know and didn't really want to find out.

After another half hour of fitful sleep I was jarred awake by a cannon shot. I lay staring into the blackness of my bag and then cautiously stuck my head out. Same still, clear night and the cold bit into my nose so that I crawled back in. The boys surely wouldn't freeze without at least letting me know, would they? I finally crawled out and into my insulated ski pants and parka and moccasins to make a check.

I was just starting out when the next cannon shot jolted me and I realized what was happening. The birch trees were splitting in the cold. It has to be minus thirty C to do that so I finally had a fix on the temperature. This time all the guys were awake and cold but not enough to want to get out and get dressed. All right. They weren't that cold then, and the polio kid was the best of all. He was cold above but not below. The pine bows were better insulation than the foam sleeping pads.

I got the tarps that we carried for windbreaks and covered the boys and crawled back in. Trees continued to crack the rest of that long night and at first light I lit the tea fire. Minutes later everyone was up and drinking hot tea. Nothing in this world can compare to hot sweet tea when you are freezing to death.

Curiously enough, the temperature rose rapidly when the sun came up and by the time we had breakfast spirits were up and the only recollection of the night was the excitement of feeling the ice shift and shake the ground and listening to the birch trees crack. What great stories to take home.

The polio kid thanked me when I dropped him off at home. No one else had ever let him try anything like that and he was tired of being treated like some kind of invalid. I told him he had the right stuff but that people would never understand. He would just have to keep doing things his own way and not let it get him down. "Just remember", I told him, "none of the people you will ever meet survived a night like you just did. You're tough and whether others know it or not doesn't matter. You know it."

The Lost Cub In The Cedar Swamp

The place where we did all our basic training for camping was a cedar swamp between Bell's Corners and Richmond, Ontario. It was located in the Ottawa green belt and wasn't as bad as it sounds. Well, nearly as bad, but not quite.

Where we actually camped was on the edge of the swamp but one of the sites the troop liked was a little rise in between water that was forested with quite respectable cedar trees. Not really big ones; those had all gone into fences and barns in the early days, and it takes a long time to regenerate a forest. This site had a running stream on one side with beaver dams and lodges, and a backwater on the other. A path led through the grove from one open field to another that had originally been farms. Follow the path for a couple of kilometres and you were in Stony Swamp; part conservation area, part limestone quarry and part encroaching industrial development. A favourite spot for a hike was to an ancient lime kiln near the quarry where history still lay exposed for the boys to marvel at. The junk lying around was fascinating, like old hand blown bottles and wagon wheels and what was left of the blasting powder magazine.

Now a cedar swamp is a curious place. This one was located on flat lying limestone, and when the beavers dammed up the little stream, backwaters formed over an area about one kilometre wide. The limestone was heavily cracked and weathered so the backwaters were not all connected on the surface. Throw in the cedar trees and undergrowth and you had a maze that could not be got through without a compass and wading up to your knees in mud.

Of course there was a trail through to the campsite but if you lost it you could forget finding it again. The camp was on the south side of the swamp and there were grassy meadows from the old pioneer homestead that had once been there. These meadows, interspersed with clumps of all sorts of shrubs and apple trees gone wild made a great playground for scout and cub games. Open space to run and bushes to hide in and make sneak attacks from.

One weekend the Bell's Corners third troop was at camp with about twenty boys. A couple of cub packs had also decided to come out for a day and they had been whooping it up for several hours, staying in the open meadows but running in and out of the swamp area as they played hide and seek games. About four in the afternoon it clouded over and all hope of guessing direction disappeared. Once beyond the first line of trees there was no way of knowing which way was which without a compass.

The troop was just in the middle of afternoon tea when a couple of cubs came to our leaders tent and asked if we had seen a cub. Well, of course we had seen several hundred of them, or at least it seemed like that. I whistled the boys in and asked the same question, which got the response "are you kidding?" We didn't think any more about it until about five when a very worried Akela came and informed us that they couldn't find one of their cubs and the cars had arrived to take them home. Our gang were now out on a wide game in the swamp, which they knew well enough to avoid getting lost. I whistled them in again but no one had seen any lost cub. Sunset was approaching and the time to panic had arrived.

As luck would have it, the troop had recently gone through instruction on how to search an area so I asked them if they would do a search just covering an area in the swamp as wide as they could and still be sure they would not miss any thing the size of a cub. Away they went and we could hear their progress from all the shouting and hollering. The Akela wanted to go too but we advised him to stay where he could go for professional help if our boys didn't find anything. He turned a bit whiter still at this suggestion but stayed put.

Half an hour later, with about an hours good daylight left the troop returned with a negative report. The Akela sent a car for the police, and I sent the troop on another sweep farther in to the swamp. There was some complaint at this because they couldn't go farther in, hold formation and still avoid wading in mud that was not too far above freezing. But scouts are scouts and away they went again. They were just returning when more cars started to arrive and we all faced the frightening prospect of a major search in the dark, when one of the scouts came tumbling into camp gasping and soaking wet yelling "we got him, we got him".

He turned and headed back into the swamp with all of us behind him. The cub had hidden in the swamp in one of their games and when he tried to come out he hit water. Not wanting to get wet he followed the edge of the water trying to go around it. Concentrating on the water he soon lost all sense of direction and when it clouded over there was nothing to tell him which way was south. He could hear the sound of voices but sound is deceiving and he couldn't find a way out of the watery trap he was in. Nobody responded to his calls, which were probably before the troop started to look for him. Finally he decided to wade through the water in the direction of voices. Unfortunately the water he picked went above his waste and never seemed to end.

Hypothermia set in and by the time scouts came near him he could no longer shout. When he heard something crashing through the bush near him he panicked and made one last effort to run. He couldn't of course but his flopping about made enough noise that the scout going by heard it and stopped to look.

Hypothermia in young kids works fast. Luckily aid was at hand by the time we carried him out of the swamp and he recovered with no ill effects. Another few minutes and he would not have made any sound, the scout would not have found him and we would all have been participants in a tragedy rather than a celebration.

A lot of cubs left with a greatly enhanced respect for scouts that day. No one came to give them hero badges but that was all right. They only did what they were supposed to do anyway, and I made sure they knew that was what heroism was all about.

The Bobcat

There are big adventures and little adventures. This one was little. It was another training camp at our cedar swamp out on Richmond Road near Fallowfield. Training camp sounds a bit wimpy but they were anything but. The cedar swamp had everything that can give you problems in winter, including rotten ice around beaver lodges and skunks that come out of hibernation occasionally in bad moods. You would be too if you had to sleep all winter in a hole in the ground.

This particular night turned cold and we had the whole troop, including many on their first winter overnight. The cars were two kilometres away which doesn't sound like much unless you are trying to get to them in the middle of the night with a sick kid in the freezing rain.

Nothing like that occurred this time but the usual problem arose after supper. The kids got cold and wanted a big campfire. Well, the camp was too close to the city for that. Most of the available fire wood had been used years before. Besides, we always taught that winter fires were not for warmth, just for cooking. You can not sleep and keep a fire going too and you need your sleep to keep your strength up.

One can get too much sleep though. In January, if you are in the sleeping bag by seven, you have to stay there for twelve hours until it is light enough to get up. Our solution to this was to go for night maneuvers that would keep everyone warm till at least nine o'clock. There are some old ruins about two kilometres from the camp site so we got everyone dressed for hiking and set off.

It works out well on a night with a full moon but at the Richmond swamp there is enough sky shine from the city lights, even in overcast, to see quite well enough for hiking. That uses up the two hours between supper and bed time and by the time everyone is tucked in there are only ten hours left till morning. Winter nights are long.

We had one boy on this camp that had a sleep walking problem which is always difficult at any time of year. All you can do is place him between others so that if he gets up someone will hopefully wake up and alert the scouters. Thompson did more than sleep walk. He was subject to nightmares and screamed occasionally like the wail of the banshee. These screams would bring the whole camp awake with their collective hairs standing on end.

The moon was full that night and it was cold and silent as only a cold winter night can be. About one in the morning I was sound asleep when a screech like I had never heard went off right in my ear. I didn't wet myself but it was a close thing.

I did rise vertically, as if by levitation, and was standing upright with my sleeping bag still zipped tight around my neck. I couldn't run of course but hopped in circles staring wildly about. Nothing. I slowly unzipped and crawled into my ski suit and moccasins and went to the group of boys where Thompson was sleeping. They were all awake except Thompson and a quavering voice said, "scouter? What was that?"

I said, "it was just Thompson having a nightmare, go back to sleep."

Another voice answered. "It wasn't Thompson, scouter. He's right beside me and I was awake. I was just going to get up to pee."

The hair stood up on my neck again.

"Stay in your bags until I check all the rest and then I'll come back and stay here while everybody gets up to pee."

Everyone was awake. It was the first all troop pee parade that I had presided over. Except for Thompson. He slept peacefully on. The boys went back to bed and the two scouters spent half an hour walking in circles around the area half expecting to come across some demented soul freezing to death in the swamp. Nothing but deathly silence and so we went back to bed wondering if a whole troop could have a collective nightmare.

It was after breakfast the next morning when two of the boys came and said they had found some tracks they didn't recognize. I went with them and stared in some disbelief at pug marks. Pug marks. That's the track left by cats. But these were big. Like the size of my fist. We tried to follow them among all the tracks left by boys and the last one we found was two metres from my sleeping bag.

I looked up my animal track book at home and it had to be either a Bob Cat or Lynx. This was on the outskirts of Ottawa and I doubt if anyone believes the story except the scouts that were there. But the Gatineau hills are just across the frozen river and the swamp has lots of rabbits in it. It is part of the green belt around Ottawa and more and more animals like fox and deer, raccoons and skunks and rabbits are showing up there. And at least one Bob Cat.

Mississippi Bloopers

Canoe Tripping

Canoe trips are always good for unexpected adventures. Wind is the big culprit in fowling up schedules. Most horror stories concerning canoe trips come from either under estimating the difficulty of rapids or trying to stick to a schedule when the wind gets too strong for the skill of the canoeists. Rain is a different sort of hazard. If you get caught in the rain you just keep paddling. In most canoe country it can rain for days and it's not much fun sitting in a tent waiting for it to stop. You might just as well grin and bear it. Wind almost always drops in the evening and even if you have to paddle in the dark and pitch camp by flashlight you can usually make up the time lost waiting for it to calm.

One of our favourite canoe trips was the Mississippi river between Mazinaw lake and Dalhousie lake. The river passes a number of really beautiful lakes, like Crotch and Mud (naming lakes appropriately is not a Canadian talent) as well as many small chutes and rapids. Enough to be exciting without undue hazard for young scouts.

Of course the difficulty depends on the water level and the Mississippi ranges from flood to trickle depending on the amount of rainfall and the time of year.

The Mis-read Rapids

One trip was made early in April with the water high and most of the bigger chutes and rapids had to be portaged, often with wet feet. Some of the smaller ones were not even visible, the water having completely submerged them. Above Crotch lake a chute which is never navigable presented a deceptively easy looking run with the water pouring over a ledge and down a thirty metre slope at an angle of about ten degrees. The surface was as smooth as glass until it entered the small pool at its base, where a standing wave about a metre high separated the slope from the calm water of the pool. Another scouter was bringing up the rear and I had already disembarked most of the scouts and started the portage.

I was loading up for the second trip when Don arrived and beached his canoe. His partner was on his first canoe trip and didn't know much about white water. Of course this water wasn't white. It was smooth and black. Even the standing wave hardly moved. It looked like a sculpture. Don looked at the chute and said that surely you could run a thing that was that smooth. I laughed and pointed out the standing wave at the bottom. Now ten degrees doesn't sound like much if you are an alpine skier, but water running down a slope like that is moving fast and there is nothing that can resist its power if it gets hold of you.

At any rate, I was half way down the portage when I heard the hollering. I dropped my pack and ran for the bottom wondering who had screwed up. I always regret not having witnessed the spectacle. Don and his partner had decided that the wave didn't look that big, so instead of unloading the canoe they went for it. Fortunately for them there was another group with an empty canoe on the far shore of the pond who saw it all and rescued them and their gear before they got swept into the second chute, a much rougher one that would have chewed them to pieces and spit them out.

The guy that rescued them described the scene for anyone who would listen. It's probably one of his favourite stories to this day. He was standing by his empty canoe and looked back up at the chute to admire the scenery just as a canoe appeared near the top. Assuming that they didn't realize how close they were to disaster he started hollering, which is what I heard. Of course Don knew what he was doing, at least until he hit the standing wave at about forty kph. As the bow punched through, water filled the canoe before the bow lifted and the canoe came through vertically completing an end over end somersault, dumping gear and paddlers into the ice cold water.

We made camp early that night to build a big enough fire to thaw and dry out two wiser canoeists. Much to Don's chagrin it was too good an object lesson to be missed so the whole troop went back to study the scene and listen to the rescuer's account which got more dramatic with each telling.

The Low Level Campsite

Another time on the Mississippi we were trying to decide where to spend the night. I favoured Crotch lake (a far more beautiful piece of real estate than the name implies) with many barren, windswept, rocky campsites, (black flies, you know) but Don liked swamps and having got lost in the meandering channels of Mud lake among the hectares of wild rice, our daylight was running out. Don had a favourite campsite just below Mud lake so he won this argument.

Apart from the hordes of mosquitoes, it looked pretty good. It consisted of dry matted organic material over a network of cedar roots and muskrat tunnels and since the water was low, the springy stuff looked like a comfortable place to spend the night. There was just enough room to get everyone in and so we applied the mosquito repellant and settled in for the night.

About midnight it started to rain. No problem. It always rains on canoe trips. But this rain had a pretty serious sound to it. About four in the morning it was still pouring down and I was just wondering how I was going to relieve myself without getting into all my rain gear when I suddenly felt wet around my hips. I put a hand down and sure enough, I was wet and I knew I hadn't done it.

Four in the morning is pitch black, so I had to rummage around for my flashlight and by the time I had it on I heard voices from the other tents. I looked out the flap and all I could see was water. The river had risen about two feet and that was enough to flood our little haven about ten centimetres deep.

"May day! May day!" I hollered. To which Don replied, "oh, shut up".

It was too late to get dressed dry and the shore line did not permit a retreat to higher ground so by the light of flashlights we broke camp, packed everything completely sodden into half swamped canoes and embarked in the dark to drift down to the first place where we could haul out above water line and try to regroup. The humour is always lost on the victims at the time, but later on, fun happenings like this provide laughs for the rest of your life.

Raccoons

A different trip in different weather provided another learning experience even for the old scouter (me). This was a gorgeous summer night camped on the bare rock above Kings Chute. The rock slopes down into a beautiful swimming hole which makes a perfect end to a hot day of paddling. The moon was full that night and we sat around the campfire long after bedtime. Fortunately black flies go to bed at sundown and mosquitoes are relatively easy to discourage.

Now the upper Mississippi has a lot of wildlife including bears and raccoons so you don't take any chances with food. Pack every food item in a separate bag which can be hoisted into the air at night over a convenient limb, at least three metres high and one metre from the trunk. Never take anything that even smells like food into the tent.

Well, we had done all that. Since I always sleep alone in a pup tent (I snore abominably and no one will sleep near me) I left my empty pack outside the flap to save space. About three in the morning I awoke to rattling and snuffling sounds and finally poked my head out. The moon made visibility excellent and there by the fire place was an immense racoon dragging my back pack towards the bush. He (or perhaps she; who can tell) ignored all my threats and even a flashlight shone in his eyes so I finally crawled out and cautiously reached out far enough to grab a trailing strap.

The racoon didn't want to give up so there we were at three AM having a tug of war over my empty back pack. I needed that pack and wasn't about to let go. In spite of growls and snarls the racoon made no attempt to come any closer than he could help and eventually we moved to within reach of a long wiener roasting stick which I grabbed and swished menacingly around making nice slicing noises in the air. This finally convinced the beast that the pack was not worth the effort and it let go and backed off a few metres.

Keeping a close eye on my friend, I found a rope and tied the pack to a limb up out of reach. When I crawled back into the tent he was still sitting there watching.

In the morning I examined the pack and found a nice hole chewed in one corner where a block of Balderson cheddar (the coon had good taste) had got too warm the previous day and melted a bit of oil into the fabric of the pack. That hole is still there to remind me that smell is enough to tempt a wild animal. Of course no one else witnessed this conflict of wills in the night and my story was met with the scepticism I suppose it deserved. The hole could have been chewed by a mouse and no one else was sleeping close enough to hear the pitched battle that had taken place.

Another racoon story in another setting illustrates the care one needs to take in dealing with these animals. This was the episode of the Troop Leader's pack. A Troop Leader is the oldest boy in the troop who has risen above the rank of Patrol Leader but has either not reached the age to go on into rovers or prefers to stay with the troop. They often turn into scouters.

This particular story took place at a regional training camp near the Quyon Ferry that crosses the Ottawa river north of Ottawa. We had a bunch of new scouts out there and the troop leaders job was to ensure that they did everything right. That included hanging all food items over branches out of reach of raccoons. Scouters with good Troop Leaders don't diminish their prestige by checking their work in front of new scouts, so the preparations for the night went unchecked. To be fair, I might not have caught it anyway.

The next morning, responding to hollering and laughing, I went to see what was up. The troop was gathered around the tree where their food had been hung and there on the ground was the remains of the Troop Leader's supplies. He had hung his pack too close to the trunk. To add insult to injury the raccoons had emptied his food bag, leaving the bag still in the tree in the offending position, and had spread all his food out neatly on the ground. They had then eaten all the meat, followed by all the desserts, cookies, candies and so forth, and left all the vegetables. The Troop Leader became a vegetarian for the weekend.

The object lesson was too good to waste so the entire camp was brought over one troop at a time to inspect the result of not hanging food properly at night. The Troop Leader's reputation was protected by saying that this was done on purpose to demonstrate the principle but whether anyone believed that is left to your imagination.

One last recollection before I sign off. I have forgotten all the detail of this one but for one thing. I had nightmares about it for many years, which I remember more clearly than the real thing.

We winter camped at Beaver Creek south of Saskatoon occasionally. The creek was fifteen miles south of the city and the road went all the way there in the summer. In the winter it was cleared of snow only to the last farm, which left about three miles to go on foot (skis, snowshoes or whatever). This was bald prairie with no escape from the wind, but the creek was a depression maybe fifty feet deep and full of poplar trees and willows. It ran roughly West so gave good protection from the north wind.

This camp followed a major blizzard so we knew we would have snow for building shelters; igloos or at least walls. So the cars dropped us off and we started the long walk on snow packed hard by the force of the blizzard winds. Everything went fine until we suddenly realized that we should be there. The creek wasn't there.

Where there should have been stands of poplar there was nothing but scrub brush and flat prairie as far as you could see. The sensation was not pleasant. Disorientation is a well known term but few people ever actually experience it. When you are young it is worse because the mind doesn't immediately conclude that some logical explanation exists. What must be, simply isn't and a feeling of panic takes hold.

Of course the answer soon became apparent. The scrub brush was the tops of thirty foot poplar trees. The entire creek valley had drifted in until it was level with the surrounding prairie. Please remember that they have in the past lost trains in Saskatchewan completely buried by drifting snow. This is not a tall tale.

We were in some difficulty because we needed the valley for protection and it wasn't available. It was also dangerous to walk anywhere near it because the snow was soft where it covered the depression and you could sink out of sight if you hit a hollow.

I don't recall the rest of that camp. Obviously we survived. But then the dreams started. Always the same dream. Walking at night to the edge of the river bank to look out over the lights of Saskatoon. But at the edge, nothing but a black void.

There is a curious sequel to this. Many years later we were living in the Credit Woodlands in what is now Mississauga when the great Eastern Seaboard power failure occurred (1968 I think). We didn't have any candles so we got in the car after an hour in the dark to go to the convenience store on Dundas. It is on a rise that lets you look out over Toronto and the display of lights of that great city is quite spectacular.

When we topped the rise we stopped. There was nothing there but a black void. The hair stood up on my head as the dream came to life. Being a rational Engineer at this time should have helped but to believe that all of Toronto could go down at the same time wasn't exactly rational. Of course the reality was a lot worse but fortunately for the sake of sanity we are only allowed a small view of our surroundings at any one time.

www.ingramcontent.com/pod-product-compliance
Lightning Source LLC
LaVergne TN
LVHW091558060526
838200LV00036B/900